The Art of Unification

Democracy or Not?

The Art of Unification

Democracy or Not?

LORENZO D. LEONARD

ELEVATE PRESS

Elevate Books
An imprint of Inspire Books

Print ISBN: 978-1-961065-37-6
e-book ISBN: 978-1-961065-38-3

PRINTED IN THE UNITED STATES OF AMERICA

For My Daughter and Son

Jennifer and Lorenzo

CONTENTS

PREFACE

*Confession of errors is like a broom
which sweeps away the dirt
and leaves the surface brighter and clearer.
I feel stronger for confession.*

—Mahatma Gandhi

I open this preface with a paraphrase of a timeless truth: "Let those among you who are without sin cast the first stone." Though this body of work speaks in depth about the importance of living with principled integrity, guided by a moral blueprint, I do not stand in judgment, nor can I, as one who has also missed the mark. I cast no stone because I, too, have faltered. For much of my life, I failed to uphold the integrity I now write about, often falling short of the honorable character it necessitates.

I have served many gods, gods representing self-interest, indulgence, and personal importance, only to discover that they have helped to lead me, time and again, to humiliation and disgrace. I cast no stone at those who walk the same path I once traveled. I know all too well the struggle of striving to be the best version of oneself while being hindered by ignorance of how to live wisely and effectively.

Rather than dedicating this work to a person, I dedicate it to a mindset, one that is both liberating and painful to accept. Trust the Confession is that mindset: the moment of reckoning where true and immediate relief begins to resuscitate the soul. It is the place where deception and fantasy die, where silence and self-examination expose the weight of poor decisions, the burden of dishonor, and the sting of lost dignity.

The Confession is not merely an admission of wrongdoing; it is the honest recognition that I did not know how to live my own life. It is the revelation that, for far too long, I sought credibility, relevance, and personal value solely from external sources. I built relationships not for genuine connections but to feel loved and appreciated. I measured my worth by validation from external sources, relying on immediate gratification to fill an ever-expanding internal void.

But the more I sought self-fulfillment externally, the further I drifted from integrity, let alone any thought of a moral blueprint. What made this realization even more painful was recognizing that the relationships I had formed were with individuals who were also in pursuit of validation and immediate gratification. Thus, power, authority, and prominence became the axis upon which our relationships revolved. Yet, through it all, I always internally felt I was a good person.

That belief, however, remained an instinct rather than a personal realization. The Confession was my reckoning—an honest acknowledgment that my sole reliance upon external sources for self-fulfillment dictated my decisions and distanced me from the person I truly wanted to become. In that moment of clarity, I understood that true integrity is not found in the eyes of others but in the silent, unwavering commitment to a higher standard.

To discover that higher standard, I searched within myself for qualities that defined admirable character. Martin Luther King Jr. spoke of the content of character, a concept I knew little to nothing about. Lacking an understanding of the inherent qualities that constitute substantive character, I had only one apparent option to define my self-perception, through my positive or negative experiences. My inability to emotionally and psychologically separate myself from these experiences distorted my self-perception. A more accurate self-perception would have allowed for the conscious act of detaching from past experiences and cultivating my identity through intentional reflection, values, and growth.

I attribute the shift, the transformation of my self-awareness, from ignorance to the pursuit of a more meaningful understanding to Martin Luther King Jr. It became my personal responsibility to transform what I instinctively knew about myself into a conscious realization. I could not blame anyone for the personal torment and suffering caused by my ignorance of the inherent gifts of character within me, for I came to realize that I was not alone in this internal struggle.

My realization extended far beyond myself. I now see my society succumbing to the same moral decay that I personally experienced. The widespread corruption, passionate disingenuous, hostile polarization, the same misguided pursuits, the same hunger for external validation, the same erosion of integrity. I have chosen to no longer stand idly by as I watch my nation, a nation that I love, drift further and further into self-destruction. I have written this book because I want to do whatever I can to help prevent our nation from collapsing from within due to moral decay. If my journey, my struggles, my failures, and my reckoning can serve as a warning and a guide, then this work has a purpose greater than myself.

We live in a civilization that has historically failed to make it a priority to educate individuals on recognizing, developing, and practicing the best qualities of character they inherently possess. It is time to develop a moral blueprint expressive of this education that serves to inspire and protect all Americans. This work is dedicated to that moment of realization, to the courage it takes to confront oneself, to the painful yet redemptive power of honesty, and to the Confession, which, though difficult, marks the beginning of true transformation.

PROLOGUE

The Performance of a Lifetime

---

*In all our searching, the only thing we've found
that makes the emptiness bearable is each other.*

—Carl Sagan

Somewhere along the way, we stopped living and started performing. Generally speaking, we have crafted roles for ourselves, not based on who we truly are as individuals, but on what we are and what we think our society wants to see. For some, it's the polished image of success: the curated résumé, the house with the right zip code, the carefully postured sensual or sexual object, or the delicately worded social media post. For others, it's power, authority, and prominence, or even struggle, packaged and sold like a brand. We have learned to market our lives the way corporations market products. Image is first, and substance optional. Unfortunately, this is not living. It's surviving on illusion.

We have become a society so fixated on how we appear to others that we have forgotten how to simply be. Somewhere between the filters and the false bravado, the truth of who we truly are as individuals has been buried. Lost is the value of authenticity, not just as a catchword, but as a moral foundation for how to live, love, and lead.

In truth, what we are really selling to one another is not just a look, but an invention, a cover-up for an internal vacuum. What is being sold is an illusion that we have it all together. That we are charming, gracious, congenial, and winning. That we are unbothered and unaffected. But beneath this veneer rests a reservoir of disingenuousness. Even poverty, even pain, has become a performance, something to showcase for sympathy, attention, or leverage. Everything is carefully organized or presented, even our suffering.

But this book is not about maintaining appearances. It's about transitioning through them. It's about confronting the illusion and asking what it has cost us, not just personally, but collectively. Because once we stop performing and begin living honestly, something powerful happens: we become capable of unification. Not the kind based on conformity or control, but on shared truth. When people are no longer posturing or pretending, there is space for real connection, and from that connection, real community.

This book is about declaring what is intrinsically real and wrestling to heal what is broken, not just in ourselves, but throughout our society. It is about discovering the truth that a meaningful life is not developed based on how we look to others, but on how honestly we live with ourselves. And when enough individuals begin to live that way, with courage, compassion, and clarity, we commence to unify. We begin to transcend performance and build something authentic together.

The common theme throughout this book is to help individuals recognize, develop, and practice the best qualities they inherently possess. When an individual begins to live from that place, when an individual embraces what is inherent within them, then the masks that once concealed this truth are no longer needed.

However, it will take courage to develop this new standard of living, not one based on status, wealth, or control, but on integrity, compassion, and a bold commitment to truth. And that kind of truth doesn't just liberate an individual self, it draws people together. This kind of truth can't be sold, only lived. It is the foundation for unification. It is the foundation for democracy, if we are brave enough to live it.

Lorenzo D. Leonard

Chapter 1

THE ART OF DEVIATION

*The present is the only time in which any
duty can be done, or any grace received.*

—C.S. Lewis

*You either walk inside your story and own it
or you stand outside your story and
hustle for your worthiness.*

—Brené Brown

Throughout history, the global community has repeatedly witnessed one faction of its collective inflicting unbearable tension, extreme wickedness, and unpleasant and repulsive violence upon another faction. The primary motivation for unleashing these extreme patterns of behavior has persistently been to achieve either outright or supplemental power, greed, and prominence. The stated narrative to justify such actions, time after time, has revolved around fabricated motives of self-interest. Reasons expressed for the forthcoming ill fate have included either a cultural clash, competition for resources, territorial disputes, or unsettled historical complaints. Also, reasons for the use of unprincipled power and violent behavior can involve differences pertaining to religious beliefs, political power and control, economic and social disparities, race, ethnicity, radicalization, and extremism.

Persecution, intolerance, discrimination, and hatred utilized to achieve absolute or additional power, greed, and prominence maintain their longevity exclusively due to the weight and staying power of intellectual, emotional, and spiritual impoverishment. The resolve to discredit or destroy the legitimacy of another individual or group to achieve any or all of the above-mentioned goals reflects a one-dimensional mindset that is grossly mistaken to satisfy self-fulfillment.

Such an outlook is nothing more than a desperate attempt to attain credibility, relevance, and value that occurs based on an internal state of deprivation. This way of life is emblematic of a will to survive that necessitates a need to pursue power, greed, and prominence over another person or group. Due to this condition of impoverishment, developing a multidimensional viewpoint that supports a system of living emblematic of unification regarding a diverse populace is not to be considered.

Internal deprivation does not encourage an individual to integrate into their thinking the words of the famous, influential Dutch post-impressionist painter Vincent Van Gogh: "Admire as much as you can; most people don't admire enough."[1] Nor will impoverishment encourage an individual to disengage from transferring feelings, attitudes, desires, or fantasies onto another person or group and embrace the visionary words of the renowned American novelist Toni Morrison: "I didn't fall in love, I rose in it."[2] Instead of pursuing empowerment, which sets in motion the development of a will to live and encourages

---

[1] Vincent Van Gogh and Ronald de Leeuw, editor, *The Letters of Vincent Van Gogh* (New York: Penguin Books Limited, 2003).

[2] Toni Morrison, *Jazz* (New York: Vintage International, 1992), 135.

others to embrace the same ideology, the impoverished pursue fragmentation, discord, and depraved partisanship.

Internal intellectual, emotional, and spiritual diminishment will exhibit either an outright dismissal or insincere recognition with respect to acknowledging another individual or group's credibility, relevance, and value. Also, in lockstep with this rebuff is the refusal to openly recognize another person or group's exceptional qualities of character, such as a strong sense of community, integrity, reliability, creativity, transparency, innate intelligence, clarity, understanding, empathy, and accountability. Nevertheless, it is important to remember that dismissal or insincere recognition relating to the triumphs of others can effortlessly be manipulated by the impoverished to give an appearance as being genuine.

This is explicitly true when recognition also must include achievements of the impoverished that prop up their self-importance and self-indulgence. For example, during a conversation when an individual is citing their personal successes or distinctive virtues in the company of a person who represents influence based on power, authority, and prominence, it is prudent to devote time to openly recognizing the successes achieved during the conversation. It is important to share the stage with an internal state of deprivation or risk reaction in the form of ridicule, patronizing, or criticism arising as a result of intense jealousy. Institutions established on a hierarchical basis—where individuals and groups are ranked one above the other based on economic standing, gender, race, education, religion, family, age, career, and employment status—are steadfast in continuing to establish this predominant pattern of living.

Due to these institutions having been founded on power, authority, and prominence, such a customary pattern of living becomes a necessary means to uphold the will-to-survive mentality. In addition, the refusal to recognize another person or group's special qualities of character outside of their specific external categorical identification is extremely important to maintain. *What* an individual is with respect to economic status, gender, race, ethnicity, and religious and political affiliations is valued more than *who* an individual is intrinsically. Again, distinctive attributes such as innate intelligence, an underlying sense of good, originality, and multiplicity are downplayed as trivial and shallow.

For the intellectual, emotional, and spiritually impoverished, maintaining leverage over another person or group is vital to their need to feel superior to others. When retaining power, authority, and prominence is at stake, this is expressly true. As previously stated, the ability to detect this behavior is easy and obvious to notice. There will persistently and consistently be a noticeable lack of regard on the part of the impoverished to avoid recognizing the admirable and sustainable attributes that comprise another individual or group's legitimacy. To do so would be considered a realistic threat for another person or group to achieve the goal of empowerment, which means attaining sustainable and genuine legitimacy.

In George Santayana's book, *The Life of Reason: The Phases of Human Progress*, he shares an insightful message. Santayana states:

> Human life, when it begins to possess intrinsic value, is an incipient (emerging) order in the midst of what seems a vast, though, to some extent, vanishing chaos. This reputed chaos can be deciphered and appreciated by man only in proportion as the order himself is confirmed and extended. For man's consciousness is evidently practical; it clings to his fate, registers, so to speak, the higher and lower temperature of his fortunes, and, so far as it can, represents the agencies on which those fortunes depend. When this dramatic vocation of consciousness has not been fulfilled at all, consciousness is wholly confused; the world it envisages (envisions) seems consequently a chaos.

Life begins to have some value and continuity so long as there is something definite that lives and something definite to live for. Here, on a small scale and on a precarious foundation, we may see clearly illustrated and foreshadowed that Life of Reason which is simply the unity given to all existence by a mind in love with the good. When definite interests are recognized and the values of things are estimated by that standard, action at the same time veering in harmony with that estimation, the reason has been born and a moral world has arisen.[3]

It is reassuring to hear another voice, Santayana's, acknowledge the importance of human life, recognizing its intrinsic value. It is also encouraging to hear Santayana endorse this emergent appreciation as a practical means to provide a more in-depth understanding of an individual's surrounding environment. That supplementary understanding involves how one's environment can be interpreted and understood to be chaotic and fragmented due to a lack of appreciation for the irreplaceable intrinsic value.

What defines intrinsic value as unique and unparalleled is the ability to correctly define personal credibility and relevance in a sustainable format. Absent an education revealing this unrivaled influence leaves an individual with no other pathway than to mistakenly pursue power, authority, and prominence as principal means to attain credibility and relevance. Under this mantle, the after-effect of going down this pathway is to end up with a sense of power, authority, and prominence that, at best, is untenable and unsustainable.

Unfortunately, this manner of achieving credibility and relevance generates a corrupt standard of living where individuals or groups of people recklessly pursue their own interests, often at the expense of

---

[3] George Santayana, *The Life of Reason: The Phases of Human Progress, English Edition* (New Delhi, India: Prabhat Prakashan, 2021), 13–15.

others. Hence, the need arises for the practices of injustice, discrimination, prejudice, and chauvinism to boost the probability of fulfilling one's own interests. This standard of living will also produce little collaboration and compassion amongst individuals or groups. A "dog-eat-dog" setting best describes this standard of living, where only the strongest or most cunning survive.

However, once the personal treasure of intrinsic value and its properties that exemplify the attributes of substantive character are embraced, an individual's life and the lives of others are of consequence, signaling a definitive unification. Reason replaces irrationality and its generated societal ills. The abuse of power for personal gain, domestic violence, gun violence, hate crimes, disparities in income and access to resources, unfair treatment or prejudice based on factors such as socioeconomic status, gender, race, ethnicity, and age are ultimately replaced. Reaching intelligent conclusions based on rational thinking, understanding, logical judgments, and making sense of experiences without initially internalizing encounters creates an ethically formed world. Suddenly, the words of the great German philosopher Friedrich Nietzsche come to life: "He who has a why to live can bear almost any how."[4]

What has hindered the education to appreciate and value one's intrinsic value is a three-thousand-year-old practice that began when the official recording of civilizations was initiated. Upon entering this life, an astonishing and debilitating societal custom starts in motion. This custom, by design, is covert, and its primary function is to disregard educating an individual to recognize, value, and practice their unique attributes that represent substantive character. Inherent credibility, as comprised of worthy attributes, describes what Santayana has termed as intrinsic value. (A detailed discussion regarding this

---

[4] Friedrich Nietzsche, *Twillight of the Idols* (Indianapolis: Hackett Publishing Group, 1997).

three-thousand-year-old practice is in the October 2023 paperback titled *Trust the Confession: Disavow Ignorance for Personal Freedom*.)

This lack of education is replaced with an intentional focus on coaching an individual through seductive visual aids to primarily pursue legitimacy through material and external sources. The ancient Greek philosopher and scientist Aristotle proposed the idea, "Nature abhors a vacuum." Aristotle believed that unfilled spaces go against the laws of nature and, therefore, will be filled with something. A team of researchers from Tulane University has suggested there are exceptions to this rule based on their own exploratory findings.[5] However, for the sake of this discussion, Aristotle's idea will suffice. When an education that represents an instructive tool to highlight a person's intrinsic value, comprised of their enriching attributes, is not acknowledged, valued, and put into practice, the consequence is predictable. This vacuum is subsequently filled with the opposite of admirable and sustainable attributes.

As earlier stated, what develops due to this impoverishment is an internal state of intellectual, emotional, and spiritual deprivation. It is this destitution that influences an individual to define themselves only by good or bad experiences. No matter what side of the experience ledger is chosen, the data internalized is flawed. When a solitary encounter or totality of encounters is directed at *what* an individual is externally or possesses materially, there is an inability to counter experiences, good or bad, with recognition of substantive qualities comprising inherent credulity and relevance.

In addition, personal behavior will consistently be motivated by a preoccupation with one's own self-importance and self-indulgence and displayed in an authoritarian and controlling manner. Relationships resemble potholed one-way streets supported by one-dimensional thinking

---

[5] Barri Bronston, "Roll Over, Aristotle, Nature Doesn't Always Hate a Vacuum," *Tulane University*, June 15, 2020, https://news.tulane.edu/pr/roll-over-aristotle-nature-doesn't-always-hate-vacuum.

with very little to no concept of what collaboration, partnership, and teamwork require. Having entered this life at a disadvantage, lacking an instructive education that assists an individual in recognizing distinctive qualities that build toward personal empowerment, a counterproductive occurrence takes place.

An intensive yearning to experience self-actualization and self-fulfillment develops, which becomes projected onto the external world. It goes without saying—this manner of fixation will impede any attempt to achieve sustainable personal gratification and contentment. Surrendering to external and material sources the responsibility for achieving credibility and relevance assigns a staggering amount of influence to an entity invested in the unscrupulous. It is important to know that such an excepting source is principally invested in attaining power, authority, and prominence by whatever means necessary. The means can include inflicting unbearable tension, wickedness, unpleasant conversation, and repulsive violence upon another individual or faction to attain the goals.

As evidence to the previous statement, entrenched throughout the annals of global history are disturbing examples of perversion that bastardize a leading principle that bolsters the quality and sanctity of human life. The prominent principle, "We hold these truths to be self-evident, that all men (and women) are created equal, that they are endowed by their Creator with certain unalienable Rights, that among these are Life, Liberty and the pursuit of Happiness," has been weakened and degraded throughout the global community's history.

This disturbing perversion is consistently established as a one-dimensional manifesto, which is the unrelenting pursuit of power, authority, distinction, and superiority. Differences that could be commemorated to nullify the history of bastardization are instead brought to bear the brunt of an evil intent—to discredit or destroy. In the Preface, we explored a grim snapshot of instances when the sanctity of human life was demonstrated to be marginalized in favor of preserving ambitions of dominance, influence, and importance; we could include with that sampling the Crusades (1096-1291), Rwandan genocide (1994), Apartheid in South Africa (1948-1994), Indian Partition (1947), Yugoslav Wars (1991-2001), Croatian War of Independence (1991-1995), the Bosnia War (1992-1995), and the Northern Ireland conflict from 1960 to the Good Friday Agreement reached in 1998.

In America, the snapshot would include violence committed against Black people during slavery (17th–19th centuries), the Jim Crow Era (late 19th–20th centuries), the civil rights movement (1950s–1960s), Chicago's Red Summer (1919), and the Tulsa Race Massacre (1921). Deep-seated racism, genocide, and discrimination committed against Native Americans involved the European colonial conquests (16th–19th centuries), Trail of Tears (1838–1839), Wounded Knee Massacre (1890), boarding schools' ruthless conditions and cultural erasure practices (late 19th–20th centuries), and the recent Dakota Protests against oil pipelines to be installed within the Standing Rock Reservation (2016–2017).

In the words of the great English playwright, poet, and actor William Shakespeare, "Love all, trust a few, do wrong to none," has become in many sectors of the world community a foregone historical example. The celebrated author and public speaker Adrian S. Potter provides an examination of the quote:

> In the opening scene of Shakespeare's comedy *All's Well That Ends Well*, a mother shares this quote with her son. It's excellent advice for any child (or anyone) getting ready to face the world on their own. Shakespeare tells us that every single person, regardless of background, is worthy of love. But he also cautions us to be wise about who we put our trust in because trust is something to be earned. While we may not be able to control the actions of others, we can control how we treat people.

If there's one rule to live by, it's to always show kindness
and never do anything to hurt others.[6]

Witnessed more recently on the international circuit is the persistent
display of destitution by two nations that have become masters of the
art of deviation, which threatens the global community's already fragile
stability. Russia and China have leveled against Ukraine and Taiwan, re-
spectively, heavy doses of repudiation to Shakespeare's statement, "Every
single person, regardless of background, is worthy of love." Legitimacy
with respect to sovereignty and territorial boundaries for both Ukraine
and Taiwan is being combatively denied by Russia and China, respec-
tively. To the credit of Ukraine and Taiwan, both countries have developed spirited societies committed to establishing prolific histories and
autonomy during intense times to develop and control their respective
international and global attributes.

Russia, for example, confidently commissioned itself to disrupt and
destroy Ukrainian lives based on two self-proclaimed narratives: cultural clash and territorial dispute. From February 20 through March 21,
2014, Russian special forces seized part of Ukraine, the self-governing
parliament and government of the Republic of Crimea. Immediately
following this limited invasion, Russia annexed Crimea. This act of
depraved aggression was immediately defended by the Russian Defense
Minister Sergei Shoigu as a need to protect the rights and "threat to
lives" regarding Russian-speaking inhabitants living in Crimea.[7] By
eight years, both acts of aggression were to preempt Russia's long-term
intention, which was to ultimately conduct a full-scale invasion of
Ukraine.

On February 24, 2022, Russia initiated a large-scale invasion of

---

[6] Adrian S. Potter, "Shakespeare's Advice for a Better Life Could Work
for You," *Medium*, November 5, 2023, https://adrianpotter.medium.com/
shakespeares-advice-for-a-better-life-could-work-for-you-b89e00e33582.

[7] "The Crisis in Crimea and Eastern Ukraine," *Britannica*, https://www.britannica.
com/place/Ukraine/The-crisis-in-Crimea-and-eastern-Ukraine.

Ukraine that signaled an attempt to resuscitate a former and tarnished identity as a Soviet powerhouse. Looking back, Russia appears to have achieved this unspoken motive. Procurement of additional power, authority, and prominence came at the expense of the death and destruction of many Ukrainian people and the country's infrastructure. This initiative to retake former Soviet territories and expand its influence officially launched the Russia-Ukraine war.

Russia's aggression against Ukraine was the first large-scale invasion to take place in a European country since World War II. Bestselling author and professor of Ukrainian history at Harvard University Serhii Plokhy states in his book *The Russo-Ukrainian War: The Return of History*: "If the collapse of the USSR was sudden and largely bloodless, growing strains between its two largest successors would develop into limited fighting in the Donbas in 2014 and then into all-out warfare in 2022, causing death, destruction, and a refugee crisis on a scale not seen in Europe since the Second World War."[8]

When one faction pursues the objective of obtaining additional power, authority, and prominence by using the art of deviation, the motive quickly becomes transparent. In Russia's case, inventing the existence of a cultural clash and territorial dispute against Ukraine exhibits an impoverished and destitute mindset on the part of the aggressor. Its manufactured, one-dimensional objective is unfailingly established to serve self-importance and self-indulgence. Its number-one form of distorted sustenance is the toxic drink of infallibility. When Defense Minister Sergei Shoigu said the country's military actions in Crimea were justified because of a "threat to the lives of Crimean civilians" and danger of "a takeover of Russian military infrastructure by extremists," evidence of Russia's sense of infallibility had clearly been digested. The transparency of the blatant lies was obvious to all outside of its influence, except those also drinking the lethal quencher of infallibility.

---

[8] Serhii Plokhy, The Russo-Ukranian War: The Return of History,

The violent aggression of annexation by Russia to make the State of Crimea a Republic of Russia, along with other sovereign territories of Ukraine, demonstrated its panic-stricken and reckless state of mind. Ukraine had benefited from successfully accomplishing the art of unification with a presidential-parliamentary system of government, its parliament's approval of its constitution on June 28, 1996, which became a public holiday. The impoverished, driven by the need to attain power, authority, and prominence for their survival, will always overreact with aggression when the empowered, once under their control, advance beyond their reach.

There is no question—Ukraine and Taiwan have different and complex histories. However, there is one important similarity that both share with one another, worth recognizing. Taiwan is being threatened by whatever means necessary to capitulate and allow China to reclaim the island as part of its territory under the "One China" policy. However, it is true that Hong Kong came under the rule of Communist China on July 1, 1997.

Amy McKenna, senior *Encyclopedia Britannica* editor with a primary focus on geography and history pertaining to sub-Saharan Africa, wrote the following article titled "Is Hong Kong a Country?" McKenna states:

> But Hong Kong is not a country. Hong Kong is a special administrative region of China. Hong Kong's status as a special administrative region stems from its history as a former British colony. By way of treaty or lease with China, the islands and mainland area now known as Hong Kong came under the control of Great Britain at various points in the nineteenth century. From that time until its transfer back to China in the late twentieth century, Hong Kong developed on a different trajectory, both politically and economically, than mainland

China—which, in contrast to Hong Kong's status as a British colony, began that period with its imperial dynasty in decline and ended it as a republic under communist rule.

Spurred by the pending expiration of a ninety-nine-year lease (1898–1997) for part of the territory, the 1984 Chinese-British joint declaration paved the way for all of Hong Kong to be returned to China. The handover occurred on July 1, 1997, at which point the Basic Law of the Hong Kong Special Administrative Region took effect. The Basic Law outlined the concept of "one country, two systems," under which Hong Kong, though now part of China, was allowed to maintain its capitalist economy and to retain a large degree of political autonomy (except in matters of foreign policy and defense) for a period of fifty years.[9]

Currently, there are two separate governing institutions claiming to be the legitimate government of China. The Republic of China (ROC) governs the island of Taiwan, while the People's Republic of China (PRC) controls the mainland and is governed by the Chinese Communist Party. According to the PRC in its adamant statement, "The Mission of the People's Republic of China to the European Union," on August 15, 2022:

> The one China principle has a clear and unambiguous meaning, there is but one China in the world, Taiwan is an inalienable part of China, and the Government of the People's Republic of China is the sole legal government representing the whole of China. The de facto basis

9   Amy McKenna, "Is Hong Kong a Country," *Encyclopedia Brittanica*, April 28, 2023, https://www.britannica.com/story/is-hong-kong-a-country.

for the one China principle is unshakable. Taiwan has belonged to China since ancient times. In 1895, the Qing government, defeated in the First Sino-Japanese War, was forced to cede Taiwan and the Penghu Islands to Japan.

After the Chinese people's victory in the war against Japanese aggression, China recovered Taiwan and the Penghu Islands, resuming the exercise of sovereignty over Taiwan in October 1945. The fact that Taiwan was returned to China is a part of the post-WWII world order. Since 1949, although the mainland and Taiwan are yet to be reunified, Taiwan's status as part of China's territory has never changed. On October 1, 1949, the People's Republic of China (PRC) was founded, becoming the successor to the Republic of China (1912–1949), and the Central People's Government became the only legitimate government of the whole of China. As a natural result, the government of the PRC should enjoy and exercise China's full sovereignty, which includes its sovereignty over Taiwan.[10]

It is not unusual that there would be a difference of opinion regarding Taiwan's sovereignty between the Republic of China and the People's Republic of China. Hong Kong was considered a special administrative region, but like Ukraine, Taiwan is considered "The Taiwan Miracle" due to its accelerated economic growth and industrialization. A key point overlooked regarding Taiwan's lawful sovereignty is similar to Ukraine's established lawful sovereignty.

---

[10] "Questions and Answers Concerning the Taiwan Question (2): What Is the One-China Principle? What Is the Basis of the One-China Principle?" *Mission of the People's Republic of China to the European Union,* http://eu.china-mission.gov.cn/eng/more/20220812Taiwan/202208/t20220815_10743591.htm

Dr. Gerrit van der Wees, former Dutch diplomat, former editor of the *Taiwan Communiqué*, and educator of Taiwan history at George Mason University, states in his February 4, 2022, article titled, "Was Taiwan Ever Part of China?"

> The Dutch East India Company originally established a presence and operated a colony on the island of Taiwan from 1624 to 1662 and 1664 to 1668. However, the Dutch presence was overtaken and dissolved by the Ming Dynasty in 1662, which was subsequently defeated by the Qing Dynasty in 1683. Taiwan remained completely under Chinese rule from 1624 to the late nineteenth century. Nonetheless, at the conclusion of the first China (Qing Dynasty) and Empire of Japan war from July 25, 1894, to April 17, 1895, Japan was awarded Taiwan as conditions set forth in the Treaty of Shimonoseki on April 17, 1895.

> By the 1920s, the island had become a prosperous model colony with a good educational system and health care, but with strict governance. During the 1920s and 1930s, neither the nationalists nor the communists cared very much for Taiwan. However, Japan would eventually lose Taiwan as a colony due to being defeated at the conclusion of World War II. Clearly, the claim, "Taiwan has always been part of China," is dubious at best. It was always at, or primarily outside, the periphery of the Chinese empire. Soon after World War II ended, the Chinese Civil War began in 1945 and ended in 1949. This internal conflict was focused on two opposing governing factions attempting to establish military control over the entire China province. The Nationalist Government (The Republic of China, ROC) and the

communists (The People's Republic of China, PRC) represented the two opposing factions.

Armed conflict began approximately in August 1927 and concluded in December 1949, with the People's Republic of China taking military control of mainland China. The Nationalist Government realized they had lost the ability to gain military control of mainland China and withdrew to control and secure the island of Taiwan. Government-wise, the nationalists governed Taiwan as a single-party state for forty years under martial law until 1987.

Also, in 1987, Taiwan began developing a democratization process, which eventually led to establishing a multi-party democracy with democratically elected presidents. The first direct presidential election occurred in Taiwan, the Republic of China, on March 23, 1996. By 2000, the Democratic Progressive Party (DPP) came to power and began to pursue Taiwanese independence and identity. Since the early 1990s, Taiwan has been a vibrant democracy that wants to be accepted as a full and equal member in the international family of nations.[11]

Both Ukraine and Taiwan were able to disengage from governments that were invested in one-dimensional strategies that opposed democratic multidimensional systems of living. The systems of living for Russia and China are principally supportive of power, authority, and prominence resting in the hands of a few. Persecution, intolerance, discrimination, and hatred are utilized by both outliers to achieve absolute

---

[11] Gerrit van der Wees, "Was Taiwan Ever Part of China," *Indo-Pacific Defense Forum*, February 4, 2022, https://ipdefenseforum.com/2022/02/was-taiwan-ever-part-of-china/.

or additional power, greed, and prominence. In their respective histories, Ukraine and Taiwan have demonstrated that within a democratic multidimensional system of living, the pursuit of power, authority, and prominence can produce differing perspectives, interests, or objectives. It is common knowledge conflict can emerge in various forms, from interpersonal disputes to large-scale societal tensions; however, when individuals or groups have differing needs, goals, values, or beliefs, the essence of conflict can surface, and hopefully, Santayana's words will come to mind: "Human life, when it begins to possess intrinsic value, is an incipient (emerging) order in the midst of what seems a vast though, to some extent, vanishing chaos. This reputed chaos can be deciphered and appreciated by man only in proportion as the order himself is confirmed and extended. Life begins to have some value and continuity so long as there is something definite that lives and something definite to live for."

At its foundation, conflict represents a challenge or obstacle to be navigated that offers opportunities for understanding, negotiation, and resolution, and this is especially true when an individual or group is educated to learn, value, and practice the attributes that comprise their intrinsic value. Going forward, it is important to understand that any system of living, be it communism, socialism, dictatorship, monocracy, or capitalism, can never rest in genuine legitimacy, security, and experience being a worthy partner of the international family of nations until the intrinsic value of its populace is at the forefront resolving the fundamental component to human interaction: conflict.

Chapter 2

A FOREGONE HISTORICAL EXAMPLE

*Probably the worst pain ever experienced is the self-
inflicted suffering that has no cure outside oneself.
To be near something beautiful or precious
but to be unable to experience it is the
subtlest possible form of torture.*

—Robert A. Johnson

*The difficult is what takes a little time;
the impossible is what takes a little longer.*

—Fridtjof Nansen

I n 1849, the French writer, journalist, and novelist Jean-Baptiste
Alphonse Karr wrote in the January issue of his journal *Les Guêpes*
(*The Wasps*), "Plus ça change, plus c'est la même chose" or "The
more things change, the more they stay the same." In other words,
in the face of appreciable changes, fundamental characteristics of the
construct remain constant. Activists and social movement enthusiasts
would acknowledge the first part of the statement as gratifying: "the
more things change." According to a Pew Research Center analysis of

government data, "Women have overtaken men and now account for more than half (50.7 percent) of the college-educated labor force in the United States. The change occurred in the fourth quarter of 2019 and remains the case today, even though the COVID-19 pandemic resulted in a sharp recession and an overall decline in the size of the nation's labor force."[12]

Also, the Pew Research Center reports:

> Women are in the majority in jobs that draw most heavily on either social or fundamental skills. The growing presence of women in higher-skill occupations helped to narrow the gender wage gap. Jobs attaching greater importance to analytical skills, such as science and mathematics, are also adding workers at a brisk pace. Women have been in the forefront of meeting these challenges, and this has been to their benefit.[13]

From Rutgers Business School, "As Title IX turns fifty years old, two generations of women have benefited from increased opportunities both on and off the field. In the pre-Title IX era, 15 percent of college athletes were women. Today, 44 percent of the opportunities to play sports go to women. Since the introduction of Title IX, three million more high school girls and two hundred thousand more college women have opportunities to play sports each year."[14] From NPR, "The

---

[12] Richard Fry, "Women Now Outnumber Men in the US College-educated Labor Force," *Pew Research Center*, September 26, 2022, https://www.pewresearch.org/short-reads/2022/09/26/women-now-outnumber-men-in-the-u-s-college-educated-labor-force/.

[13] Rakesh Kochhar, "Key Findings on Gains Made by Women Amid a Rising Demand for Skilled Workers," *Pew Research Center*, January 30, 2020, https://www.pewresearch.org/short-reads/2020/01/30/key-findings-on-gains-made-by-women-amid-a-rising-demand-for-skilled-workers/.

[14] Lisa Kaplowitz, "Title IV Increased Opportunities for Women Athletes, But There's Still More Work to Do," *Rutgers Business School*, June 23, 2022, https://www.business.rutgers.edu/business-insights/title-ix-increased-opportunities-women-athletes-theres-still-work-do.

Supreme Court of the United States declared same-sex marriage legal in all fifty states on June 26, 2015."[15] And from NBC News, "Researchers at the Yale Program on Climate Change Communication found that Americans are more worried about climate change now than they were in 2010, and support for renewable energy has also grown over time."[16] On a global scale, awareness and concern about climate change has grown significantly, which introduced an international agreement labeled the Paris Agreement, adopted in 2015.

Though the "the more things change" in Karr's statement is evidenced in our current era, activists and social movement enthusiasts would acknowledge the second part of the statement, "the more they remain the same," as being disturbing. According to the Pew Research Center, "Not all economic indicators appear promising. Household incomes have grown only modestly in this century, and household wealth has not returned to its pre-recession level. Economic inequality, whether measured through the gaps in income or wealth between richer and poorer households, continues to widen."[17] Societal afflictions, including economic inequality, have increased with the breach between the rich and the poor being more concentrated at the top. In the Human Rights Watch 2000 report:

> The United States stated that "overt discrimination" is "less pervasive than it was thirty years ago" but admitted it continued due to "subtle forms of discrimination" that "persist[ed] in American society." The forms

[15] Bill Chappell, "Supreme Court Declares Same-sex Marriage Legal in All Fifty States, *NPR*, June 26, 2015, https://www.npr.org/sections/thetwo-way/2015/06/26/417717613/supreme-court-rules-all-states-must-allow-same-sex-marriages.

[16] Denise Chow and Chase Gain, "Americans Are Warming to Climate Change—But They Can't Agree After That," *NBC News*, January 25, 2024, https://www.nbcnews.com/science/environment/americans-are-warming-climate-change-cant-agree-rcna135131.

[17] Juliana Menasce Horowitz, Ruth Igielnik, and Rakesh Kochhar, "Trends in Income and Wealth Inequality," *Pew Research Center*, January 9, 2020, https://www.pewresearch.org/social-trends/2020/01/09/trends-in-income-and-wealth-inequality/.

of discrimination reported to the United Nations by the United States included "inadequate enforcement of existing anti-discrimination laws"; "ineffective use and dissemination of data;" economic disadvantage experienced by minority groups; "persistent discrimination in employment and labor relations;" "segregation and discrimination in housing" leading to diminished educational opportunities for minorities; lack of equal access to capital, credit markets and technology; discrimination in the criminal legal system; lack of adequate access to health insurance and health care; and discrimination against immigrants, among other harmful effects. The United States also noted the heightened impact of racism on women and children.[18]

And according to the USA Facts report, "The number of reported hate crimes—crimes motivated by bias against someone's race, color, religion, national origin, sexual orientation, gender, or gender identity—rose by 7 percent between 2021 and 2022, according to updated 2022 hate crime data from the FBI. Black and/or African American people were the most frequent targets overall. Among gender-motivated hate crimes, anti-transgender hate crimes increased 35 percent year over year. Religiously motivated hate crimes increased 27 percent, and specifically, antisemitic hate crimes increased by 36 percent from 2021 to 2022."[19]

The Pew Research Center reports the following:

> Despite women's advantages in skills and education, the gender wage gap persists and is ubiquitous. Regardless

[18] "Racial Discrimination in the United States," *Human Rights Watch*, August 8, 2022, https://www.hrw.org/ report /2022/08/08/racial-discrimination-united-states/human-rights-watch/aclu-joint-submission.

[19] "Which Groups Have Experienced an Increase in Hate Crimes?" *USA Facts*, December 14, 2023, https:// usafacts.org/articles/which-groups-have-experienced-an-increase-in-hate-crimes/.

of the classification of occupations—by skill type or the importance of a skill—women's earnings fell short of men's earnings in 2018. For example, women in occupations with the greatest need for analytical skills earned $33 per hour, 88 percent as much as the men who earned $38 per hour in similar jobs. Women in occupations with the least need for analytical skills earned 82 percent as much as men in the same jobs. The wage gap persists even though women currently hold an edge over men in certain skills and in schooling.[20]

The Pew Research Center also adds to "the more they remain the same" discussion, in a report titled "Women and Leadership."

So why, then, are women in short supply at the top of government and business in the United States? According to the public, at least, it's not that they lack toughness, management chops, or proper skill sets. Instead, topping the list of reasons, about four-in-ten Americans point to a double standard for women seeking to climb to the highest levels of either politics or business, where they must do more than their male counterparts to prove themselves. Similar shares say the electorate and corporate America are just not ready to put more women in top leadership positions. As a result, the public is divided about whether, even in the face of the major advances women have made in the workplace, the imbalance in corporate America will change in the foreseeable future.[21]

[20] Kochhar, "Key Findings."

[21] "Women and Leadership," *Pew Research Center*, January 14, 2015, https://www.pewresearch.org/social-trends/2015/01/14/women-and-leadership/.

There are explicit reasons why, in the face of appreciable changes, fundamental characteristics of the construct remain constant; hence, "the more things change, the more they remain the same." An anonymous person once stated, "Those individuals advocating for change with respect to limiting the proposed negative impact stemming from societal afflictions are the most resistant to personal change. It is comprehensible that a person would feel empathy, passionate, and troubled regarding the enormity income, wealth, gender, educational, and housing inequalities impact so many individuals within this rich and resourceful nation. The same feelings of discomfort could also arise regarding racial, healthcare, sexual orientation, disability, and immigration disparities."

It is reasonable for one human being to feel compassion, incensed, and agitated about another human being's societal misfortunes. There is a limit, however, to experiencing sensitivity so that one's own position of privilege and entitlement does not weaken. To advocate for extensive and encompassing changes that could impact unaffected individuals with a reduction or loss of their power, authority, or prominence is enough reason to pause and suspend such efforts. A quick exit by the unaffected is generally accompanied by the disclaimer, "I am sorry to hear about your exact misfortune. But I wasn't there years ago when the inequality or disparity initially took place. I can't be held responsible for denying you of your rights." This scenario is especially true when the unaffected individual or others stand to lose privileges or benefits derived from the status quo.

Even though feelings of compassion arise when reminded of the unkind realities linked to social inequalities and disparities, what has never traditionally failed to be transparent is the predictable result. Wealthy individuals, corporations, political elites, and individuals representing established power, authority, and prominence based on gender, race, education, and landownership will never jeopardize the loss of eminence to elevate the credibility, relevance, and value of the pedestrian.

Conversely, historically and during the modern era, there are individuals and groups willing to reduce their eminence for the sake of fostering a more inclusive, diverse, and harmonious community. Unfortunately, this level of involvement has never garnered enough populace support to change the statement, "the more things change, the more they remain the same," to "the more things change for the principle-based improvement of humanity, the more opportunity to progress towards community unification."

The late Indian lawyer, anti-colonial nationalist, and political ethicist Mahatma Gandhi offered a prophetic statement that would certainly elevate the back half of the statement, "the more they stay the same." Gandhi stated, "Be the change that you wish to see in the world." But in order for Gandhi's statement to be acted upon, a vast number of the masses would have needed to be exposed to an educational program that taught its inhabitants to recognize, value, and practice qualities that comprise their intrinsic value. The jewels encompassing intrinsic value are revealed through the attributes that depict substantive character. Integrity, empathy, resilience, courage, dependability, authenticity, and accountability exemplify a few of the gemstones necessary to possess in order to "be the change that you wish to see in the world." Gandhi's statement spoke directly to the individual and groups who have experienced personal empowerment as a result of recognizing, accepting, and practicing their jewels of intrinsic value.

Then again, individuals and groups reluctant to accept the prophetic statement choose to remain casualties of a characterless system of living. It remains soulless, due to its intentional neglect to educate its inhabitants about the best inherent attributes they entered this life individually possessing. Thus, with this endless loyalty to an unsympathetic system of living, the door is open to becoming a willing casualty to intellectual, emotional, and spiritual impoverishment.

What is established in the absence of developing an appreciation and development of intrinsic value are hierarchical systems where individuals and groups are ranked one above the other based on economic standing, gender, race, ethnicity, education, religion, family, career, employment status, and age. What is of interest is how a sizable portion of the populace quickly adapts and develops a shared knowledge and intentional acceptance. Commonly shared and consciously accepted are injustice, cruelty, economic and gender inequalities, racism, ethnic cleansing, ageism, and homophobia—inescapable symptoms that arise from a broken and ill-fated system of living.

Even when face-to-face with this degrading understanding, the bottom line does not change. Still, no one of the impoverished state is willing to give up their distinctive awards, titles, and prizes that represent the attainment of power, authority, and prominence. Sadly, there are individuals and groups who will adamantly oppose the idea to "be the change that you wish to see in the world." The basis for the adamant opposition rests on the proverb, "a bird in the hand (power, authority, and prominence) is worth two in the bush (going against the mainstream of society with an identity yet to be determined)." Backing up that proverb is another anonymous statement: "Why should a person experience the pain of being authentic, when they can experience perfunctory acceptance more easily?" And yet, another anonymous statement comes to mind:

> If an individual is to experience 'being damned for doing,' which accompanies a system of living based on power, authority, prominence, and never being enough, or 'damned for not,' which is certain to escort the journey to claim the jewel of intrinsic value that represents attributes of substantive character, then 'damned for not' is the personal choice.

On the other hand, without a reputable societal custom designed to educate an individual to develop personal empowerment, in its place a fundamental life pursuit shifts to attaining power, authority, and prominence to achieve legitimacy. The assertion that "those individuals advocating for change with respect to limiting the negative impact stemming from societal afflictions are the most resistant to personal change" reveals itself as true when the advocate becomes victimized by a Machiavellian motive. Any effort by an advocate to motivate another person or group to make a behavioral change to limit negative conduct representing a societal disorder, while at the same time exhibiting the behavior in question, exposes the intentions of a well-designed ruse.

The reasons provided to support the advice of eliminating economic, gender, racial, ethnic, and age biases, hate crimes, and violence are sensible and practical. The advocate corroborates the idea with the fact that this type of behavior is demeaning and debilitating toward the victim. Also, corroborated is the likelihood of this behavior generating a backlash such as retaliation in the form of violence and verbal confrontation. In the moment, the individual or group receiving this advice can view this outreach as helpful and well meaning. There is one significant problem, however, that arises with this tactic that essentially establishes a one-dimensional stratagem. The advocate is not capable of leading their life by example of change outside of the cautionary speech. "Do as I say, not as I do" is the point of emphasis. External changes to address economic, gender, racial, ethnic, and age biases, hate crimes, and violence mean very little so long as the internalized biases, violence, and hate crimes continue to be perpetuated from within a group.

This tactic remains one-dimensional because the individual offering the advice has done nothing to stop demonstrating their own economic, racial, and gender biases toward the same groups. This is a classic example of how internalized classism, sexism, racism, violence, and other forms of social inequalities and disparities are perpetuated from within a group. The opposed memorialize the economic, gender, racial, ethnic, and age biases, hate crimes, and violence occurring outside the group. This clever use of ruse is to mask and distract from initiating an equivalent change to take place within the various economic, gender, and racial groups that is being encouraged to take place on an external basis. Again, this one-dimensional strategy is to continue exhibiting power, authority, and prominence over people that chiefly includes one's group of identification.

As previously stated, lacking an established societal custom designed to educate an individual to develop personal empowerment through the recognition and value of attributes comprising inherent credibility, "the more things change, the more they remain the same." Regretfully, one-dimensional strategies, rather than multi-dimensional strategies, will widen the range of inequalities and disparities motivated by impoverishment. When change is based on multi-dimensional approaches, however, the statement that "those individuals advocating for change are the most resistant to personal change" is deemed no longer an issue and a reflection of impoverishment, but rather empowerment. Useful conflict that materializes when an individual is transitioning from impoverishment to empowerment is avoided and thus projected outward in the forms of pretense and betrayal.

George Santayana shares an insightful message in his book, *The Life of Reason—or the Phases of Human Progress*. Santayana states:

> True society, then, is limited to similar beings living similar lives and enabled by the contagion of their common habits and arts to attribute to one another, each out of his own experience, what the other actually endures. What enables men (women) to perceive the unity of nature is the unification of their own wills. A man (woman) half asleep, without fixed purposes, without intellectual keenness or joy in recognition, might graze about like an animal, forgetting each satisfaction in the next and banishing from his frivolous mind the memory of every sorrow; what had just failed to kill him would

leave him as thoughtless and unconcerned as if it had never crossed his path.

Such irrational elasticity and innocent and improvidence would never put two and two together. Every morning there would be a new world with the same fool to live in it. But let some sobering passion, some serious interest, learn perspective to the mind, and a point of reference will immediately be given for protracted observation; then the laws of nature will begin to dawn upon thought.[22]

As mentioned at the close of Chapter 1, a fundamental component to human interaction is the experience of conflict. Adjusting to differences is always a challenge, especially when there is the absence of an education to recognize, value, and practice qualities that comprise a person's intrinsic value. As earlier stated, conflict can occur when making the personal choice to be "damned for not" pursuing society's marketed pathway to legitimacy, which is the attainment of power, authority, and prominence. The pursuit instead of an individual's personal jewel of intrinsic value allows an individual to learn they are intellectually, emotionally, and spiritually complete and enough. This experience is in contrast to society's espoused form of achieving legitimacy where a person learns they are never quite enough and complete. There is always more power, authority, and prominence to attain, which encourages a person to continuously chase the imaginary "carrot" of fulfillment. This erroneous code of belief generates an ugly conclusion that conflict is to be viewed as intolerable grounds to tread upon as perceived by the impoverished. Santayana recaps: "A man (woman) half asleep, without

---

[22] George Santayana, *The Life of Reason—or the Phases of Human Progress* (Legare Street Press, 2022), 40, 32.

fixed purposes, without intellectual keenness or joy in recognition, might graze about like an animal."

Conflict arising from a person's pursuit to take ownership of their individual jewel of intrinsic value is understood to be an intimidating challenge. This is especially true when breaking free from a societal norm that contends legitimacy is defined by how much power, authority, and prominence a person can achieve. Recognition, value, evolution, and practice of an individual's intrinsic value subsequently discloses how conflict, whether internal or external, can divulge important and inspiring information about oneself. However, this is only possible if the process is allowed to evolve to its natural conclusion. If an individual can identify undeveloped attributes comprising their inherent credibility, new and invigorating insights about oneself can be experienced. In addition, the new insights about oneself open the door to experience the same with respect to other people with differences.

This process can generate new and unique protocols of communication in which judgment and attempts to change the other are absent. Shared similarities can nurture a distinctive intimacy. The sharing of singular and common values, as well as habits, can contribute to a genuine interaction and affinity. Conversely, when credibility and relevance are defined by how much power, authority, and prominence a person can achieve, there is also an immense resistance to learning and embracing what is authentic about one's own self. There is little latitude in the corporate suite, in the home, and in the prayerful church for the authentic and unfeigned while chasing the infamous "carrot," which is a major theme with all three.

The personal choice to be "damned for not" pursuing society's marketed pathway to legitimacy provides an individual with the opportunity to experience being complete and enough without pursuing the never-satisfying "carrot." The purpose of conflict is to magnify undeveloped and honorable attributes comprising a person's inherent credibility. With respect to relationships, this learning process can help to view conflict as a teacher, as well as create an internal reservoir of that which is good, competent, and worthy. This process can also replace previously internalized negative self-perceptions that hinder the improvement of self. Leo Tolstoy once stated, "Nothing needful can be poured into a vessel full of what is useless. We must first empty out what is useless."[23]

It is important to remember one certainty when breaking free from a societal norm that contends legitimacy is defined by how much power, authority, and prominence a person can achieve. A threat can arise from within an individual, from an external source, as well as from both directions when taking the initiative to achieve personal empowerment. It is essential to understand the nature of a taxing conflict, which is learning to recognize and value undeveloped honorable qualities comprising an individual's inherent credibility.

For example, when breaking free from restrictive and suffocating societal norms to experience personal empowerment, one significant quality to recognize and develop is *authenticity*. To honor personal values and objectives with vulnerability helps immensely to experience inner strength. Another quality to recognize and develop would be *resilience*, which helps to maintain a focus on achieving the goal of personal empowerment in spite of the appearance of adversity and potential setbacks. Qualities that are recognized and developed such as *courage, decisiveness*, and *compassion* are extremely useful when living life aligned with your personal empowerment.

There are numerous examples throughout history when the core component of conflict was made transparent. This visibility generally brought about a conviction that human life was worth the courageous

---

[23] Leo Tolstoy, *Letters on War* (Essex: The Free Age Press, 1900), 39.

effort to preserve and to protect inherent credibility, relevance, and value. With that said, conspicuously absent from history chronicles is a *foregone historical example* that took place between Arab and Jewish communities that captured an unforgettable moment when conflict was resolved in a manner that benefited both cultures. One such effort stands out as an exceptional example when *what* an individual is simply did not matter. Economic standing, professional status, gender, race, ethnicity, religious order, or age differences were set aside to protect the sacredness of human life from the brutal intentions of evil.

Intertwined with this unforgettable moment is the disheartening Arab and Jewish conflict that depicts conflict at its most painful. It is unfortunate this tragic history has overshadowed a narrative that portrays both communities as considerate and charitable towards one another. This *foregone historical example* consists of self-sacrificing individuals devoted to confronting the underlying core of conflict by safeguarding humanitarian principles under the harshest conditions. An Arab community decided to uphold the words of the ancient Greek scholar and philosopher Epicurus: "The greater the difficulty, the more the glory in surmounting it." Amazingly, these acts of courage were conducted to preserve another culture's actual existence, which was in complete defiance to the wishes of an intellectual, emotional, and spiritually impoverished tyrant.

During World War II, just as these historic worldwide tensions and violence were taking place on the battlefield, the global community also witnessed an amazing display of humanistic and compassionate efforts to render aid and comfort to an affected culture defined as collateral damage. Initially, Italy had occupied Albania in 1939, but would eventually fall and surrender in 1943 to Allied armies from different countries who were opposed to the Axis powers, consisting of Nazi Germany, the Empire of Japan, and the Kingdom of Italy. Upon Italy's capitulation, German forces took control of Albania and occupied the country from September 1943 until November 1944.

The intent by Arab communities from the beginning of the German forces' occupation of Albania was to protect and aid Jewish communities from being impacted by hostile tensions, violence, and certain death. Surprisingly, the invading German forces were overwhelmed by a defiant opposing force. During the early stages of the German occupation, the manifestation of an old saying attributed to various anonymous sources made its presence known and affirmed the dedication by Arab communities to achieve an ambition to aid and protect. "Never make the mistake of assuming the person of peace is unskilled at war." The extract from this conflict, whether choosing to preserve life or comply with the commands of death, provided an interval of time for growth as it affected two diverse cultures. Activists, religious figures, and non-religious persons provided the global community with a winning methodology that was based on a multi-dimensional strategy devoted to protecting more than one culture.

This approach took precedence over an enemy committed to destroying any and every individual standing in its path to achieve a single-minded, one-dimensional victory; the opposite approach was evoked. The tactic that distinguished these self-sacrificing individuals from the perpetrators of power, authority, and prominence was based on a profound definition of moral justice, which included the desire to mitigate suffering. These individuals risked their own lives to offer comfort and safety to victims whose only transgressions were differences with respect to race, ethnicity, religion, economics, and customs. This call to uphold humanitarian principles was against the stringent demands and threats of death to end such efforts made by their respective tribes. Allied forces led by Britain, the United States, the Soviet Union, France, and Albanian resistance would eventually eradicate the Nazi occupation.

During the Nazi occupation of Albania, however, sixty-five Albanian Muslims demonstrated numerous acts of heroism and humanitarianism to save "nearly all of the 2,000 Jews in Albania from the furnaces of Auschwitz." The acclaimed American photographer and activist Norman H. Gershman spent five years taking photos and collecting the daring and breathtaking Albanian stories that are publicized in his book titled *Besa: Muslims Who Saved Jews in World War II*. Dr. Mordecai Paldiel, a leading scholar on the rescue of Jews during the Holocaust and author of *The Righteous Among the Nations: Rescuers of Jews During the Holocaust*, states in the foreword to Gershman's book:

> In Albania, when a person gives you Besa to act in a certain way, then he is committed to abide by it whatever the circumstances This was coupled with another inherently Albanian folk principle that of giving refuge to someone in need of help. Survivors relate that Albanians vied with each other for the honor of sheltering the fleeing Jews, a phenomenon unheard of in other European countries under the heel of the Nazis. This Islamic behavior of compassion and mercy celebrates the sanctity of life and a view of the other, the stranger, as indeed one's own close family member.[24]

Madam Jehan Sadat, the First Lady of Egypt, was married to Anwar Sadat on May 29, 1949. Just prior to the marriage, the soon-to-become president of Egypt was released from confinement due to his intense resistance of British occupation of Egypt. The marriage lasted until her husband's assassination on October 6, 1981. After an extended absence from public life to focus on her personal loss and grief, she returned to the communal stage. Mrs. Sadat resumed her life with a robust

---

[24] Dr. Mordecai Paldiel, "Foreword," in *Besa: Muslims Who Saved Jews in World War II*, Norman H. Gershman (New York: Syracuse University Press, 2008).

commitment to educate, lecture, and establish an inexhaustible presence as a social activist promoting women's rights and international peace.

At the University of Maryland, Mrs. Sadat earned the distinction of being recognized as an associate resident scholar where The Anwar Sadat Chair for Development and Peace was established and fully endowed in 1997 to honor her husband's legacy. Jehan Sadat died on July 9, 2021, at the age of eighty-seven, having accentuated her life with prominence as an Egyptian human rights activist. As follows, in Madam Jehan Sadat's human rights activist voice she commented regarding Gershman's book: "Through the eyes of Norman H. Gershman, we can see that beyond our individual identities and desires, there is a common core of self, an essential humanity whose nature is peace, whose expression is thought, and whose action is unconditional love."[25]

The entrenched custom of recognizing the value of an individual's inherent credibility and relevance regardless of gender, race, or religious order worked extremely well for saving Jewish lives by Albanian Muslims. This belief and custom became a principal motivator for devising different schemes to hide refuge Jews from Nazi German capture and subsequent execution. Top priority was given to harboring Jewish families in urban and rural locations, designing false documents that identified refugees as Albanian Muslims, and establishing escape routes to the countryside or mountains to keep out of Nazi authorities' detection. To help with the success of protecting the fleeing Jews, Albanian resistance often provided German authorities with false and misleading information, community solidarity, and an unwavering commitment to religious tolerance.

Still, the one attribute that made all of this resistance successful is explained on the inside cover of Norman H. Gershman's book. It states: "Besa is a code of honor deeply rooted in Albanian culture and incorporated in the faith of Albanian Muslims. It dictates a moral behavior

---

[25] Madam Jehan Sadat, "Endorsement," in *Besa*.

so absolute that nonadherence brings shame and dishonor on oneself and one's family. Simply stated, it demands that one take responsibility for the lives of others in their time of need." The Albanian Muslims represent the Bektashi Order or Bektashism. This religious order is a Sufi Islamic creed that symbolizes the most liberal form of Shiites.

The Bektashi Order has a long mystic tradition in Albania that originated in the thirteenth century. It is named after the Saint Haji Bektash Veli. The Albanian Bektashi Order is led by the head of the creed under the title of Baba. Gershman quotes the Baba in his book when asked to explain the Bektashi Order. The Baba expounds: "We Bektashi see God everywhere in everyone. God is in every pore and every cell; therefore, all are God's children. There cannot be infidels. There cannot be discrimination. If one sees the good face, one is seeing the face of God. God is beauty. Beauty is God. There is no God, but God."[26]

On August 30, 2009, National Public Radio host Liane Hansen interviewed Norman Gershman to discuss his book. During the interview, Gershman added: "Under the Nazi occupation, the foreign minister of Albania was a Bektashi. And he sent out a secret message to all Bektashi that the Jewish children will sleep in the same bed as your children. The Jewish children will eat the same food as your children. The Jewish children will be your family."

Toward the end of the interview, Gershman responded to Hansen's question: "What effect did this project have on you?" He replies with an answer that all of humanity can individually embrace and reject the continued bastardizing of the truth.

> Listen, I photograph with my heart. In this particular case, clearly I'm a Jew. I'm a lay Jew. But I also have studied over the years with the Sufis. And the Sufis, those are the mystical side of Islam. The Islam I know is the Islam of beauty, of music, of dance, of poetry. I don't recognize this Islam that I read about in the papers.

[26] Gershman, *Besa*, xvi.

So, it was a journey that I did with my heart. And it just reinforces that there are more good people in the world, far more good people in the world than terrorist or terrorist sympathizers. There are well over a billion Muslims. They're good people. Unfortunately, in the media you rarely read or hear about the good people. I found the good people in Albania.[27]

Teach an individual to recognize, welcome, value, and practice their inherent credibility that comprise meritorious qualities of character they innately bring into this earthly existence, and the means to corrupt or debase principles deemed genuine become insignificant. Contemptible impoverishment used to bastardize the creed, "We hold these truths to be self-evident, that all men (and women) are created equal, that they are endowed by their Creator with certain unalienable Rights, that among these are Life, Liberty and the pursuit of Happiness," loses power, authority, and prominence to divide humanity due to erroneous information that purely serves self-interest.

Nothing more needs to be said, except closing with Akbar Ahmed's Introduction chapter in Norman H. Gershman's book:

Along with Christianity, Judaism and Islam constitute the three 'Abrahamic' religions—that is, religions descended from the prophet Abraham. The commonality of many of their basic values is a message that is sorely needed today. We are often guilty of looking at our own faith in juxtaposition, or in opposition, to the other faiths and assuming exclusivity. 'We are the purest, the best,' we too often tell ourselves. For me, as an anthropologist, that assumption is a myth, because there is no such osmosis, synthesis, and overlap among the faiths.

---

[27] "The Muslims Who Saved the Jews," hosted by Liane Hansen, Weekend Edition Sunday, *NPR Radio*, August 30, 2009, https://www.npr.org/templates/story/story.php?storyId=112384539.

Norman's study of the Albanian example here is testimony to an Islamic type of behavior utterly different from those so unfortunately making the headlines these days. It is a record of acts, not of vengeance, hatred, and suicide, but of compassion, kindness, and help to persons of another faith and origin. I hope that the example of the Albanian rescuers will serve as a role model inspiring others, Muslims and followers of other faiths, to walk in their footsteps and be truly human beings when faced with similar moral challenges. We as a world civilization are at the crossroads. Building these bridges across religions and cultures is no longer an intellectual pastime; it is an imperative if we are to survive the twenty-first century.[28]

The art of unification demands attention, not only of the American populace but also of the global community as we cross over the river of humane denial onto the ocean shores of personal empowerment, remembering the words, "be free to live your life, with your life." This form of unification affords humanity an opportunity to finally advance the age-old saying, "the more things change, the more they remain the same," to "the more things change, the more we can look forward to the elevation change can bring into our lives."

---

[28] Gershman, *Besa*, xv.

Chapter 3

CONTINUE THE DISGUISE OR NOT

*The chief danger in life is that you may
take too many precautions.*

—Alfred Adler

*That virtue we appreciate is as much ours as another's.
We see so much only as we possess.*

—Henry David Thoreau

François de La Rochefoucauld (September 15, 1613–March 17, 1680) was an accomplished French moralist of the era referred to French Classical literature. He once stated, "We are so accustomed to disguise ourselves to others that in the end we become disguised to ourselves." Digging deeper into the mechanics of this provocative statement, it is quite understandable why the need to conceal oneself from others would occur in the first place. When a system of living establishes a norm that credibility, relevance, and value are based on *what* an individual is in terms of external status and material possessions, self-betrayal becomes a likelihood. Then, to establish a compatible norm that supports amassing power, authority, and prominence as viable means to boost credibility, relevance, and value, self-betrayal becomes a customary choice to live one's life.

This act of exploitation that takes place is understating the recognition, development, practice, and well-being linked to *who* an individual is regarding the substantive qualities that comprise their intrinsic credibility. To dedicate one's life to the pursuit of credibility, relevance, and value primarily through external achievements and material possessions necessitates the need to wear a disguise. The purpose of this camouflage is to conceal as much as possible the obsession with accruing power, authority, and prominence. By committing to this way of life, an individual chooses a path where authenticity, accountability, integrity, compromise, and forgiveness are viewed to be fundamentally irrelevant, indicative of weakness, and vulnerable to the certitude of rejections—the genuine is simply not regarded as possessing credibility and relevance.

Only when a breach of trust or crisis has struck as a result of poor judgment, which usually involves the lack of a moral compass, will there be a revelation regarding the absence of developed qualities representative of substantive character. This happens, for example, when a civic leader, clergy, trustworthy elected politician, or appointed government official is exposed for nullifying their credibility by accepting monetary bribes, gifts, or sexual favors for personally advancing the interests of another nation or corporation aspiring to gain power, authority, and prominence.

Within a system of living that limits personal legitimacy to an external status and material possessions, the inability to demonstrate with confidence one's genuine individuality and self-worth in the face of trepidation remains a difficult task to effectively move past. As a consequence of the lack of faith and conviction pertaining to the value and strength associated with *who* an individual is, disguising oneself to others as well as to oneself becomes inevitable. Qualities representative of substantive character derived from intrinsic credibility—and deemed vulnerable, irrelevant, and indicative of weakness—are suppressed. When there is distrust with respect to the importance of demonstrating sound character, and that mindset inhibits the display of mutuality, authenticity, accountability, and compassion, the act of self-exploitation and self-betrayal has materialized.

When credibility, relevance, and value are primarily derived from external sources, and amassing power, authority, and prominence are practiced in order to boost legitimacy, collateral damage can be expected. With these two prominent norms deeply embedded within a system of living, the adverse impact upon the populace increases with the influence of a third morally debilitating norm. Reinforcing personal credibility based strictly on external sources and amassing power to boost legitimacy is the age-old degenerate norm that helps to solidify anti-social symptoms. Since its existence, humanity has incessantly been plagued with racism, injustice, socioeconomic inequality, discrimination, gender inequality, crimes of passion, mass gun violence, hate crimes, contentious political division, and more.

This age-old and well-established norm is a custom that a person has one option available to define their self-perception. Lacking a comprehensive understanding of an individual's totality, which includes the devalued intrinsic credibility, experiences become the lone benchmark to develop self-perception. In addition, an individual is also left with no other option than to internalize being either a failure, inadequate, and inept or successful, adequate, and proficient based on positive or negative experiences. Because there is an internal void concerning personal knowledge of the attributes representing substantive character as derived from intrinsic credibility, the outcome is predictable. An individual will find it extremely difficult to separate emotionally, intellectually, and spiritually from experiences primarily due to a lack of awareness of their totality. Within a system of living that equates external status and material possessions with legitimacy, successful, adequate, and proficient experiences require power, authority, and prominence to sustain a successful self-perception.

On the other hand, experiences concluding with failure, inadequacy, and ineptness will generate a negative self-perception. With very little to no personal information to offset either positive or negative self-perception, the door swings open for various addictions, mental health issues, and a deeper dive into a state of impoverishment. With a more intense relationship with impoverishment, the more pronounced is the need for a disguise. No matter how skillful and talented an individual is with respect to wearing their disguise, those benefiting from power, authority, and prominence will never consent to recognizing a coalition of equals.

All partaking in the charade understand there is no trust to be developed amongst other pretenders. No manipulation of words can honestly suggest that an act of unification is possible while these three prominent norms maintain a vice-like grip on a populace. This is especially true when a populace is willing to hide from their genuine credibility while showcasing various disguises. The effort to justify the use of power, authority, and prominence to provide the appearance of unification would simply be the endeavor to legitimatize an abstract version of freedom rather than actual independence.

Often trivialized and undervalued, attributes derived from an individual's inherent credibility would provide the type of clarity necessary to understand an individual's totality is determined by more than an accumulation of experiences, good or bad. As François de La Rochefoucauld previously stated, "We are so accustomed to disguise ourselves to others that in the end we become disguised to ourselves." Failure to understand and appreciate *what* we are externally and seeing accumulated material possessions as just a microcosm of a person's totality prevents the South African Anglican Bishop, theologian, and human rights activist Desmond Tutu's words from being understood. Desmond Tutu states: "My humanity is bound up in yours, for we can only be human together." He speaks directly of the human interconnectedness and the power of mutual care and reverence. The art of unification is established through the qualities representing substantive character as they are recognized, developed, valued, and practiced because this aspect of a person's life is what links all of humanity together through one common thread of good.

Then again, so long as the authentic is determined to be a sign of weakness, irrelevant, intellectual, emotional and spiritual impoverishment will continue to adversely dominate the human landscape. Humanity will be divided with the power of mutual care and reverence a mere vagueness of thought. Negative influences impacting the personal agenda are further affirmed so long as substantive character is cheapened and marginalized by the need to wear a personal disguise. It is little wonder why relationships, casual, exclusive, and primary by their nature, will transition over a period of time into hostile and adversarial war zones. This transition is usually in stark contrast to the honorable desires originally hoped for in the beginning phases of the association. However, deception and cunning are undeniably considered viable means to an end when it comes to establishing relationships based on a personal investment to attain power, authority, and prominence.

This investment undermines respectable credibility and legitimacy achieved through principled behavior. Only clergy, ministers, attorneys, and therapists dare tread into this emotional and spiritual impoverishment to salvage the broken hearts that have fallen victim to an indistinct and misdirected masquerade party. The resentment and retribution for not maintaining their disguise can be brutal, as so many expectations have been erected on the premise of pretense. But with a way of life that principally values what an individual is externally and materially, how can the process produce different results? This result is confirmed by François de La Rochefoucauld, when he states: "True love is like ghosts, which everybody talks about, and few have seen. No persons are more frequently wrong, than those who will not admit they are wrong."

The problem with establishing a relationship with an individual who is invested in a way of life that primarily values *what* an individual is externally and materially is how much is required in order to have that alliance. First and foremost is the expectation to preserve and protect the self-importance and self-indulgence so that credibility and relevance are never jeopardized or diminished in terms of external status and material value. The personal and spiritual sacrifice made to have such an alliance is far too much to surrender, particularly when the likelihood of being cast overboard for any slippage looms on the near horizon. A relationship based on *who* an individual is intrinsically, where the qualities of character truly matter, can be more stable and does not require any personal and spiritual sacrifices. Self-importance and self-indulgence have no place in this relationship, especially when integrity, civility, and dignity count for the character of this coalition.

A way of life that principally values *who* an individual is intrinsically in terms of the attributes that represent admirable character will also acknowledge an importance regarding *what* an individual is externally and materially, but not as its fundamental value of an individual. This dual recognition seeks to achieve three specific and purposeful deeds: balance, stability, and virtue. To value and mark with distinction the merits of character will neither necessitate nor create the counterproductive need to wear a personal disguise. Authenticity is always pressing forward to establish transparency as an essential and necessary means to achieve what can truly feed the human soul: an unwavering and consistent link to itself and its surroundings. Authenticity, which is one of the many attributes of sound character, is also expressive of the empowerment derived from its demonstrative abilities. When understood in terms of an actual benefit, to discard the disguise in favor of what truly sustains life in a vigorous and meaningful manner, the hesitant or faint of heart need not apply.

David Brooks, a Canadian-born American conservative political and cultural commentator, has been an author and editor since 1986 and has written for *The New York Times* since 2003 and the *PBS NewsHour* since 2004. Mr. Brooks has also taught at Yale University and is a member of the American Academy of Arts and Sciences. In October 2023, Mr. Brooks published his #1 *New York Times* bestselling book, *How to Know a Person: The Art of Seeing Others Deeply and Being Deeply Seen.*

Dave Brooks states on page sixteen: "I'm hoping this book will help you adopt a different posture toward other people, a different way of being present with people, a different way of having bigger conversations. Living this way can yield the deepest pleasures." On the front fold of the cover, he observes, "There is one skill that lies at the heart of any healthy person, family, school, community organization, or society: the ability to see someone else deeply and make them feel seen—to accurately know another person, to let them feel valued, heard, and understood."

The front cover continues to provide a brief synopsis, which reads:

> And yet we humans don't do this well. All around us are people who feel invisible, unseen, misunderstood. In *How to Know a Person*, Brooks sets out to help us do better, posing questions that are essential for all of us: If you want to know a person, what kind of attention should you cast on them? What kind of conversations should you have? What parts of a person's story should you pay attention to?
>
> *How to Know a Person* helps readers become more understanding and considerate toward others, and to find the joy that comes from being seen. Along the way it offers a possible remedy for a society that is riven by fragmentation, hostility, and misperception. The act of seeing another person, Brooks argues, is profoundly creative: How can we look somebody in the eye and see something large in them, and, in turn, see

something larger in ourselves? *How to Know a Person* is for anyone searching for connection and yearning to be understood.[29]

David Brooks tackles an extremely complex and provocative subject concerning *How to Know a Person*. He describes an inability of people to see one another on a deeply felt level and to feel as though they have been seen, valued, and understood. Brooks meets head-on the desire to accurately know another person, to let the other person feel valued, heard, and understood. There is no question as to Brooks' scholarship, intelligence, and genuine desire to address the countless individuals here at home and throughout the global community who feel invisible, unseen, and misunderstood. There is no question as to his assessment of the hostility, fragmentation, and misperception eroding the basic moral foundation of society. David Brooks takes a bold step forward to champion the art of unification by addressing the intellectual, emotional, and spiritual impoverishment that is severely suffocating the moral advancement of this society and evidenced in other societies.

In my previous book, titled *Trust the Confession: Disavow Ignorance for Personal Freedom* and released in October 2023, Chapter 7 begins with a lesson in reasoning. Sir Arthur Conan Doyle, the renowned British writer and creator of the popular fictional character Sherlock Holmes, uses deductive reasoning to aid the unrivaled detective in solving mysteries. Holmes was famous for disclosing the importance of being able to reason backwards to resolve what, on the surface, may appear at first glance extremely complicated. For example, in Sir Arthur Conan Doyle's mystery, *A Study in Scarlet*, a forthcoming revelation begins when Watson (Holmes's trusted crime-fighting companion) states to his friend, "Holmes, how did you solve this mystery with so many unscripted developments?"

---

[29] David Brooks, *How to Know a Person: The Art of Seeing Others Deeply and Being Seen* (New York: Random House, 2023).

Holmes calmly replied:

> My dear friend Watson, in solving a problem of this
> sort, the grand thing is to be able to reason backwards.
> That is a very useful accomplishment, and a very easy
> one, but people do not practice it much. In the every-
> day affairs of life, it is more useful to reason forwards,
> and so the other comes to be neglected. There are fifty
> who can reason synthetically for one who can reason
> analytically . . . Let me see if I can make it clearer. Most
> people, if you describe a train of events to them, will tell
> you what the result would be. They can put those events
> together in their minds and argue from them that some-
> thing will come to pass. There are few people, however,
> who, if you told them a result, would be able to evolve
> from their own inner consciousness what the steps were
> which led up to that result. This power is what I mean
> when I talk of reasoning backwards, or analytically.[30]

Inductive reasoning involves starting from specific premises and
forming a general conclusion that addresses current conditions, while
deductive reasoning involves using specific premises to reason backwards to form a specific genesis. As just stated, David Brooks is profoundly aware that "normal times" are beyond the reach of this nation.
As a concerned human being with all the good intentions, sincerity, and
honesty, David Brooks addresses what he experiences as this nation's
social crisis. He states:

> I've been writing as if we live in a healthy cultural envi-
> ronment, in a society in which people are enmeshed in
> thick communities and webs of friendship, trust, and

---

[30] Arthur Conan Doyle, *A Study in Scarlet: A Detective Story* (New York: Ward, Locke,
Bowden, and CO, 1892), 215.

belonging. We don't live in such a society. We live in an environment in which political animosities, technological dehumanization, and social breakdown undermine connection, strain friendships, erase intimacy, and foster distrust. We're living in the middle of some sort of vast emotional, relational, and spiritual crisis. It is as if people across the society have lost the ability to see and understand one another, thus producing a culture that can be brutalizing and isolating.

The thing we need most is relationships. The thing we seem to suck at most is relationships. The effects of this are ruinous and self-reinforcing. Social disconnection warps the mind. When people seem unseen, they tend to shut down socially. People who are lonely and unseen become suspicious. They start to take offense when none is intended. They become afraid of the very thing they need most, which is intimate contact with other human beings. They are baffled by waves of self-loathing and self-doubt. After all, it feels shameful to realize that you are apparently unworthy of other people's attention. Many people harden into their solitude. They create self-delusional worlds.

Sadness, lack of recognition, and loneliness turn into bitterness. When people believe that their identity is unrecognized, it feels like injustice—because it is. Loneliness thus leads to meanness. As the saying goes, pain that is not transformed gets transmitted. In our society, we confer huge amounts of recognition on those with beauty, wealth, or prestigious educational affiliations, and millions feel invisible, unrecognized, and left out.[31]

---
[31] Brooks, *How to Know*, 97, 99, 100.

From David Brooks' book, it is clear that he is invested in the idea of societal unification, which speaks volumes to the depth of his character. He uses inductive reasoning to remedy the division, antagonism, abuse of power, and authority ravishing the very soul of this nation. Throughout his book, numerous suggestions are provided to help in the art of seeing others deeply and being deeply seen. For example, treat attention as an on/off switch, not a dimmer; be a loud listener; favor familiarity; make them authors, not witnesses; don't fear the pause; do the looping; the midwife model; don't be a topper. There is undeniably great advice when engaged in "Hard Conversations" and the importance of knowing the other person's background.

Throughout the second half of David Brooks' book, he makes available an incredible number of personal and professional examples when conflict arises at the center of a relationship. What is also just as incredible are the insights he proposes to his reader that will assist in how to respond to the various conflicts. Every suggestion sets the stage to know a person, how to see another person, and at the same time be seen by the other person. At the beginning of his book, Brooks establishes his podium and conviction with a moment of brutal honesty. Brooks states:

> Some days it seems like we have intentionally built a society that gives people little guidance on how to perform the most important activities of life. As a result, a lot of us are lonely and lack deep friendships. It's not because we don't want these things. Above almost any other need, human beings long to have another person look into their face with loving respect and acceptance. It's that we lack practical knowledge about how to give each other the kind of rich attention we desire.
>
> I'm not sure Western societies were ever great at teaching these skills, but over the past several decades, in particular, there's been a loss of moral knowledge. Our

schools and other institutions have focused more and more on preparing people for their careers, but not on the skills of being considerate toward the person next to you. Human beings need recognition as much as they need food and water. No crueler punishment can be devised than to not see someone, to render them unimportant or invisible.[32]

There is absolutely no question as to David Brooks's intention to experience our system of living elevated to a morally acceptable level where all the various groups of people will benefit. Even though Brooks' contention is predominately built on the platform of inductive reasoning, there is complete agreement with him as he so aptly details the underlying present premise. The current problem facing this nation is its rapid moral decline into the depths of intellectual, emotional, and spiritual impoverishment. Brooks confirms this agreement with the following:

> As the years have gone by, I have increasingly fixated on what I see as a deeper cause of our social and relational crisis. Our problem, I believe, is fundamentally moral. As a society, we have failed to teach the skills and cultivate the inclination to treat each other with kindness, generosity, and respect. 'Moral formation' is really about three simple, practical things. First, it is about helping people learn how to restrain their selfishness and incline their heart to care more about others. Second, it's about helping people find a purpose, so their life has stability, direction, and meaning. Third, it's about teaching the basic social and emotional skills so you can be kind and considerate to the people around you. In a sense,

---

[32] Brooks, *How to Know*, 8–9.

American culture became demoralized. Moral talk and moral categories gradually came to occupy a smaller role in American life.[33]

The system of living that David Brooks expresses great concern about regarding its lack of moral education did not just begin since World War II, as he suggests. Brooks quotes B. Edward McClellan from his book *Moral Education in America*: "By the 1960s deliberate moral education was in full-scale retreat. Educators who had once prided themselves on their ability to reshape character now paid more attention to the SAT scores of their students, and middle-class parents scrambled to find schools that would give their children the best chances to qualify for elite colleges and universities."

Again, Sherlock Holmes reminds the curiosity seeker, "The grand thing is to be able to reason backwards."[34] This reasoning will provide insight as to how and why the current conditions exist. Holmes adds, "In the everyday affairs of life, it is more useful to reason forwards, and so the other comes to be neglected."[35] As this response pertains to this subject matter, the other that is neglected involves discovering the genesis of the moral decline and the opportunity to change its basis for existing. The act of unification will need to include deductive reasoning, or else "the more things change, the more they remain the same." Here is where David Brooks and this writer have differences as two concerned individuals desirous to address this nation's moral decline. Brooks offers several valid suggestions that, on the surface, make a great deal of sense. Nonetheless, his suggestions are slanted toward behavioral changes, which establishes credence for "the more things change, the more they remain the same."

---

[33] Brooks, *How to Know*, 104–105.

[34] Doyle, *A Study*, 215.

[35] Doyle, *A Study*, 215.

It is important to move beyond the surface and behavioral changes so that attention can be directed internally where the indispensable quality or essence of an individual exists. Elevate the hearts and minds through a process that educates an individual to know the best characteristics they inherently possess, and the act of unification has a chance to succeed. Once a person learns to value these attributes, it is natural to want another person to enjoy learning to value their totality as well. With this process added to personal development, behavioral suggestions made by David Brooks, lawmakers, and civic leaders are easily adopted. The reason for the adoption success is due to there already being a baseline in existence comprised of substantive characteristics. This change occurs because the internal composition is recognized and valued as an integral component of one's totality.

Without this internal transformation taking place, an individual will be rearranging their external disguise relentlessly to accommodate surface changes. This avoidance is to circumvent an in-depth personal examination. Again, when credibility, relevance, and value are solely derived from external sources and amassing power, authority, and prominence to boost legitimacy, avoidance of qualities emerging from a personal examination deemed irrelevant, indicative of weakness, and vulnerable are suppressed. In spite of this tactic, there is a price to pay for this avoidance, which can silently set in motion an inevitable collision with oneself. This collision can produce an internalized sadness, loneliness, depression, hostility, and anger. When projected outward, these emotions become the basis for the symptoms of socioeconomic disparity, gender inequality, racism, injustice, discrimination, mass gun violence, hatred, political discord, and more to dominate a culture.

To pursue behavioral changes, rather than instinctive changes that typify an innate underpinning of substantive morality, immortalizes "the more things change, the more they remain the same." This has been the historically preferred method for crafting laws in an attempt to curb societal ills that produce turmoil and discord amongst the populace. To some degree, outward restraint has been gained. Nevertheless, relying on this manner to construct laws that confront symptoms that reflect a state of impoverishment has been unsuccessful in elevating the hearts and minds of the populace. It is essential to understand the ultimate source of glory with a system of living that bases legitimacy exclusively derived from external sources is the accumulation of power, authority, and prominence. Complying with the values of such a system generates life to the haunting words of François de La Rochefoucauld: "We are so accustomed to disguise ourselves to others that in the end we become disguised to ourselves." Authenticity is eagerly sacrificed for the accumulation of power, authority, and prominence.

Samual Noah Kramer's masterfully written book titled *The Sumerians: Their History, Culture, and Character* was published in 1963 by The University of Chicago Press. As a result of years absorbed in dedicated study, earlier publications, and this specific body of work, Kramer has rightly distinguished himself as a leading expert in Sumerian history and language. Making use of Kramer's examination and findings regarding the Sumerian civilization creates the opportunity to reason backwards to around 4000 BCE. The purpose is to understand the genesis of the moral discrepancies that have negatively impacted successive civilizations. What is known about the Sumerian civilization is especially impressive. This culture is recognized for its diverse population of people, infrastructure, markets, educational institutions, writing, variety of economic prospects, cutting-edge agriculture, and elaborate political and religious institutions. To this day, the Sumerians remain distinguished as the pioneers of advances that have led ensuing civilizations to follow within their province and beyond. Kramer is able to capture the scanty and limited beginnings of the Sumerian civilization. He states:

> Sumer, the land which came to be known in classical times as Babylonia, consists of the lower half of Mesopotamia, roughly identical with modern Iraq from

north of Baghdad to the Persian Gulf. Its climate is extremely hot and dry, and its soil, left to itself, is arid, windswept, and unproductive. The land is flat and river-made, and therefore has no minerals whatsoever and almost no stone. Except for the huge reeds in the marshes, it had no trees for timber.

Here, then, was a region with "the hand of God against it," an uncompromising land seemingly doomed to poverty and desolation. But the people that inhabited it, the Sumerians, as they came to be known by the third millennium BC, were endowed with an unusually creative intellect, and a venturesome, resolute spirit. In spite of the land's natural drawbacks, they turned Sumer into a veritable Garden of Eden and developed what was probably the first high civilization in the history of man.[36]

The resemblances between the early Sumerian system of living and many modern-day systems of living, which include this nation, are rather revealing with respect to understanding the genesis and evolution of inequity and inequality. There is no question as to the ingenuity, resoluteness, and courage demonstrated by the populace to take barrenness and turn it into fertility. However, Sumerian society, with its driven external ambitions and acquisition of material resourcefulness that influenced their religion, education, and character, would be the first recorded civilization to be deficient in establishing an equivalent or parallel moral foundation. Comparisons with the past and present systems of living, which include motivations, are informative. Kramer helps to interpret:

---

[36] Samuel Noah Kramer, *The Sumerians: Their History, Culture, and Character* (Chicago: University of Chicago Press, 1963), 3.

Although the leading deities were assumed to be ethical and moral in their conduct, the fact remained that, in accordance with the worldview of the Samarians, they were also the ones who in the process of establishing civilization had planned evil and falsehood, violence and oppression—in short, all the immoral and unethical modes of human conduct.[37]

(For additional information regarding the Sumerian religion, which includes the creation of goddesses and gods, refer to the book *Trust the Confession: Disavow Ignorance for Personal Freedom*, written by this author.)

The Sumerian school's original goal was what we would term "professional," that is, it was first established for the purpose of training the scribes necessary to satisfy the economic and administrative needs of the land, primarily, of course, those of the temple and palace. This continued to be the major aim of the Sumerian school throughout its existence. Education was, of course, neither universal or compulsory. The greater part of the students came from the wealthier families; the poor could hardly afford the cost and the time which a prolonged education demanded.[38]

Patriotism, love of country, and particularly love of the home city, was a strongly moving force in Sumerian thought and action. Love of the city-state naturally came first in time and was never altogether superseded by love of Sumer as a whole.[39]

---

[37] Kramer, *The Sumerians*, 125.

[38] Kramer, *The Sumerians*, 230–231.

[39] Kramer, *The Sumerians*, 261.

Closely allied to the love of life was the value put on material prosperity and well-being. The Sumerians highly prized wealth and possessions, rich harvests, well-stocked granaries, folds and stalls filled with cattle large and small, successful hunting on the plane and good fishing in the sea.[40]

But in spite of their lofty ideals and sublime ethics, the chances are that the Sumerians could never have come as far or achieved as much either materially or spiritually, had it not been for one very special psychological drive which motivated much of their behavior and deeply colored their way of life—the ambitious, competitive, aggressive, and seemingly far from ethical drive for pre-eminence and prestige, for victory and success . . . the will to superiority, the driving ambition for victory over a rival, was a pervading source of motivation in the Sumerian behavior.[41]

One of the more powerful advances the Sumerians established has remained intact today and has become a dominant custom for humanity to struggle with throughout its history. The custom is personal credibility, relevance, and value being primarily linked to external status and material resources. To enhance this legitimacy with the attainment of power, authority, and prominence can negatively impact other individuals and groups of people. Hierarchical classifications adversely affect economic, social, gender, race, ethnicity, and age differences. Such classifications are necessary to reassure positions of power, authority, and prominence. As a major derivative of this custom, positive and negative experiences are used to define self-perception.

---

[40] Kramer, *The Sumerians*, 263.

[41] Kramer, *The Sumerians*, 264.

From the Sumerian period to this present era, there is no indication to suggest that a system of living predicated on external status and material resources that defined credibility, relevance, and value also included educating a person to learn of their individual totality. If this had taken place, then individual credibility, relevance, and value would have been expanded to include a person's inherent credibility as comprised of attributes expressive of their substantive character. Emerging from this moral education, awareness and development would have made it possible to define self-perception by more than empirical experiences.

There are various reasons why the Sumerian civilization eventually collapsed. Climate change, the ongoing attrition of fertile fields, the overuse of resources, and the economic downturn all played different roles in the collapse. Then again, the events that surely aided the collapse were the continued social conflicts that occurred within the Sumerian civilization over resources, territory, and ineffective governance that eventually made the culture vulnerable to outside invasions from the empires of Akkadians and later the Babylonians.[42,43]

However, the focus here is not on the Sumerian civilization's collapse. Instead, the focus is on a system of living this first recorded civilization began with that has continued to exist throughout the global community, including this nation. Courageous and bold efforts like David Brooks' book deserve to be taken seriously by a reader who can move beyond making external alterations regarding behavior to fearless changes of their heart and mind through an internal examination. The French moralist, François de La Rochefoucauld, if he were still with us and given another opportunity, would state, "We are not accustomed to disguise ourselves to others that in the end we remain unveiled to ourselves."

---

[42] "Ur III in Decline," *Britannica*, https://www.britannica.com/place/Mesopotamia -historical-region-Asia/Ur-III-in-decline.

[43] "Ancient Sumerian Civilization: History and Facts," *Ancient Civilizations World*, February 6, 2017, https://ancientcivilizationsworld.com/sumerian/.

The opportunity to expand upon a three-thousand-year system of living to include the legitimacy of an individual's inherent credibility, which is the principal component of an individual's totality, is awaiting humanity's embrace. *What* a person is in terms of external status and material wealth is important, but this limited standing will never be more distinctive and boundless than *who* a person is in relation to the attributes that comprise inherent credibility. The art of unification demands the latter part of this statement to emerge if humanity is to move past the last three thousand years of disguising ourselves to ourselves.

Chapter 4

UNIFICATION AND
LA AMISTAD

He who has a why to live for can bear almost any how.

—Friedrich Nietzsche

*I wish that every human life might
be pure transparent freedom.*

—Simone de Beauvoir

The unification of this republic begins with an acknowledgment that the fragmentation of its populace has reached new heights that threaten to dissolve, though an abstract freedom, this nation's fragile democracy. The populace has disintegrated into two separate camps, which, based on their observable behaviors, are antagonistically opposed to one another. Each group's conceptual thinking is distinguished as Nationalist and Loyalist rather than American. The attempt to take this nation back into its history of origin when women, Black, Brown, Indigenous, and poor white Americans suffered spiritually, economically, intellectually, emotionally, and physically due to ambiguity surrounding the Declaration of Independence is quite apparent.

Currently, that list of marginalized groups has expanded to include people with physical or mental disabilities, gender non-conforming and transgender persons not in accordance or agreement with prevailing norms, standards, or customs, immigrants and refugees, the elderly, religious minorities, and individuals with a criminal record. As a result of this obscurity and latent contradiction between the principles of liberty and equality as espoused in the Declaration of Independence, this nation has reached a defining moment of clarification. Either unification or its opposite will determine if this republic is for the people, by the people, or one self-declared special group of people.

If "We the People of the United States, in order to form a more perfect Union, establish justice, ensure domestic tranquility, provide for the common defense, promote the general welfare, and secure the blessings of liberty to ourselves and our posterity"[44] is the goal, the pathway is crystal clear. The migration toward unification will necessitate creating a new system of living that espouses a coalition of equals rather than the pursuit to continue establishing inequities and inequalities that represent empire-building. The coupling of inherent and external credibility will be a welcomed marriage that allows this republic to move from boosting an abstract freedom to humbly representing a freedom of actuality.

It is regretful this nation's populace has been exposed to "We hold these truths to be self-evident" rhetoric when this pronouncement was meant to only apply to the aloft group of men that formed this nation in its beginning. This group, the Founding Fathers of this nation, strictly equated credibility, relevance, and value with power, authority, and prominence. This is no surprise to anyone since credibility, relevance, and value have excluded the inherent credibility of a person regardless of economic status, educational credentials, gender, race, ethnicity, and age from the beginning of recorded history.

---

[44] "The Constitution of the United States," *National Archives*, https://www.archives.gov/founding-docs/constitution.

The sad truth is that Americans have never had an unencumbered beginning, having been set as rivals against one another from the beginning of this republic due to the bastardization of the truth. The dumbing down of the Declaration of Independence in order to satisfy self-importance and self-indulgence is a reminder of the French philosopher, writer, social theorist, and feminist activist Simone de Beauvoir's opening desire: "I wish that every human life might be pure, transparent freedom."[45] The American novelist, poet, and social activist Alice Walker's statement, "No person is your friend who demands your silence or denies your right to grow,"[46] is a cautious reminder when living within a system established primarily on equating credibility, relevance, and value with power, authority, prominence.

The need to reestablish this separatist mentality has just begun with the effort to forbid and outlaw trustworthy accounts and publications that expose the intellectual, emotional, and spiritual impoverishment that generated the division in the beginning, which is a dreadful mistake. Suppression motivates the same destitution of thought to recreate the fragmentation. Until personal legitimacy is taught that an individual's inherent credibility as comprised of qualities exemplifying substantive character reveals an equivalent importance as external credibility, the necessity to expose destitution of thought will accompany this journey. Unification of this nation's populace will depend on a willingness to expose the immoral consequences directly related to intellectual, emotional, and spiritual impoverishment.

Bastardization of the truth as revealed through accurate and reliable history is gaining momentum within this nation. For one example, there exists strong opposition to educating students to African American history relative to this nation, which would encompass the existence of slavery, segregation, and systemic racism. States such as Alabama, Arizona,

---

[45] Simone de Beauvoir, *The Blood of Others* (Michigan: Bantam Books, 1974).

[46] Alice Walker, in *Book of African American Quotations* (New York: Dover Publications, 2011), 179.

Arkansas, Idaho, Iowa, New Hampshire, Oklahoma, Tennessee, Texas, Utah, and West Virginia have signed into law policies that restrict or discourage educators from discussing this topic in depth or from using certain materials that have been deemed "divisive" or "controversial" by lawmakers or school boards. For example, Florida Governor DeSantis was in the news again for signing specific legislation labeled the Individual Freedom Act, also known as the Stop WOKE Act, meant to prohibit the teaching of critical race theory. As of November 1, 2022, sixteen states have passed laws (specific legislation) restricting the ability of educators to talk about race and racism in the curriculum.[47]

There are numerous arguments to justify banning this information from the educational curriculum. A few of the contentions range from a lack of importance in comparison to a more in-depth and complex American history, the information being unnecessary to a larger student audience, a political agenda as the chief motivation, and the intention to perpetuate victimhood and guilt.[48]

The renowned philosopher, essayist, poet, novelist, and prominent thinker of the twenty-first century, George Santayana, has this to say about expunging our past in his book *The Life of Reason or the Phases of Human Progress*:

> Progress depends on retentiveness. When change is absolute, there remains no being to improve, and no direction is set for possible improvement; and when experience is not retained, as among savages, infancy is perpetual. Those who cannot remember the past are condemned to repeat it. In the first stage of life, the

---

[47] Sterling Johnson, "Legislating Black History," *Harvard Law Bill of Health*, April 10, 2023, https://blog.petrieflom.law.harvard.edu/2023/04/10/legislating-black-history/.

[48] Rashawn Ray and Alexandra Gibbons, "Why Are States Banning Critical Race Theory?" *Brookings*, November 2021, https://www.brookings.edu/articles/why-are-states-banning-critical-race-theory/.

mind is frivolous and easily distracted; it misses progress by failing in consecutiveness and persistence. This is the condition of children and barbarians, in whom instinct has learned nothing from experience. In a second stage, men are docile to events, plastic to new habits and suggestion, yet able to graft them from original instincts, which they thus bring to fuller satisfaction. This is the plane of manhood and true progress. Last comes a stage when retentiveness is exhausted and all that happens is at once forgotten; a vain, because unpractical, repetition of the past takes the place of plasticity and fertile readaptation. In a moving world, readaptation is the price of longevity.[49]

It is essential to a person's well-being to be acquainted and receptive to the information conveyed by Santayana before callously moving to fulfill an agenda motivated by self-importance and self-indulgence. The move to expunge an indispensable component of American history would prove to be devastating as a consequence of being propelled by intellectual, emotional, and spiritual impoverishment. Such a move would continue to plunge this nation into a more profound fragmentation and hostile environment. Why? "Those who cannot remember the past are condemned to repeat it." States that have signed into law policies that restrict or discourage educators from discussing or teaching African American history are falling prey to an old proverb: "cutting off one's nose to spite one's face."

To suspend or stop teaching trustworthy accounts and publications that expose the distressing consequences of impoverishment has only one intended purpose. The opportunity to recreate the actions to

---

[49] George Santayana, *The Life of Reason or the Phases of Human Progress* (Independently Published, 2018), 68.

discredit or destroy another person or group arising from racism, as well as from gender and socioeconomic disparities, are the intended purposes of power, authority, and prominence "run amok." And it is with certainty that as the ban on African American history is exploited by the impoverished, the movement will eventually transition to adversely impact women and other human targets of socioeconomic disparities. Deficient in the instruction and appreciation for inherent characteristics such as integrity, humility, accountability, fairness, compassion, reliability, and empathy creates an internal vacuum regarding good and iniquitous behavior.

Societal ills indicative of symptoms representing an internal condition of intellectual, emotional, and spiritual impoverishment are displayed through power, authority, and prominence "run amok." Violence, harassment, discrimination, injustice, inequality, inequity, erosion of rights, dehumanization, and polarization must locate their human targets, or else the impoverished will devour their own. "Cutting off one's nose to spite one's face" enters the equation when the pursuit of credibility, relevance, and value is linked with amassing power, authority, and prominence to gain positions of superiority.

"Cutting off one's nose" is the intent to harm and diminish another individual or group's inherent value to gain a sense of dominance. The consequence, "to spite one's face," materializes by creating a way of life obsessed with the need to control, insecurity, ambiguity, distrust, fear, uncertainty, incapacity to appreciate simplicity, and the amount of time devoted to disguising these frailties with a maximum effort to gain more power, authority, and prominence. In spite of this, the individual determined to engage in this self-destructive behavior to "cut off their nose to spite their face" must be prepared to descend much further down into intellectual, emotional, and spiritual impoverishment. Then the question becomes, "What price glory?"

The complete history of this nation has transitioned a populace into offender and offended. Its chronicles deserve to be sought after to help prevent the repetition of yesterday's horrors. The inherent credibility and relevance of the previously mentioned offended marginalized groups have a right to be resurrected through the education of a complete and uncompromised historical account. Such a changeover allows this nation to have an opportunity to move beyond the reaches of ignorance and prejudice.

Once more, it becomes necessary to contemplate Santayana's wisdom. He states:

> The theory that all real objects and places lie together in one even and homogeneous space, conceived as similar in its constitution to the parts of extension of which we have immediate intuition, is a theory of the greatest practical importance and validity. That the unification of nature is eventual and theoretical is a point useful to remember. What enables men (women) to perceive the unity of nature is the unification of their own wills.

> A man (woman) half asleep, without fixed purposes, without intellectual keenness or joy in recognition, might graze about like an animal, forgetting each satisfaction in the next and banishing from his (her) frivolous mind the memory of every sorrow; what had just failed to kill him (her) would leave him (her) as thoughtless and unconcerned as if it had never crossed his (her) path.

> Every morning there would be a new world with the same fool to live in it. But let some sobering passion, some serious interest, lend perspective to the mind, and a point of reference will immediately be given for

protracted observation; then the laws of nature will begin to dawn upon thought. Every experiment will become a lesson, every event will be remembered as favorable or unfavorable to the master-passion.[50]

During the early stages of American history, there existed an indispensable chapter, among many other important chapters, that was managed with the "greatest practical importance and validity" and provided "sobering passion, serious interest that lent perspective to the mind." The March 9, 1841, United States Supreme Court case, United States v. Amistad, 40 US 518, was the historical moment that captured the full attention of this nation and the international community. This important chapter also ushered into this period of time a needed emphasis regarding the importance of justice for all people, establishing a stronger opposition to slavery, the fight for freedom, human dignity, and the need for unification between a divided populace. Helping to make this chapter historic was a disquieted international community, fifty-three African citizens, devoted northern abolitionists in the United States, a former president of the United States, and the judicial branch of the United States government, which included lower courts and the Supreme Court.

The following is a condensed account of the Amistad story released through the White House Historical Association:

> Illegally seized by Portuguese slave hunters in Sierra Leone, a group of Africans were forcibly brought to Havana, Cuba. Pedro Montes and Jose Ruiz, two Spanish plantation owners, purchased fifty-three individuals and set off for home. The enslaved rose up in rebellion, killed the captain, and took control of the ship. They demanded that Montes and Ruiz return them to

---

[50] Santayana, Life of Reason, 32.

Africa, but the two men steered northward. Eventually, the Washington, an American brig, seized the schooner and escorted it to New London, Connecticut. President Martin Van Buren believed that the Africans should be extradited to Cuba and hoped to do so quietly through the naval courts at the request of the Spanish government, but northern abolitionists caught wind of the incident and began raising funds to defend the enslaved.

The key issue in the case was the status of the Africans on board—were they free, or were they property? Montes and Ruiz argued that they were the rightful owners; Lieutenant Thomas R. Gedney, commander of the vessel that captured the Amistad, requested salvage rights as compensation; and legal counsel for the Africans maintained that these individuals were born free and illegally kidnapped. The District Court ruled that the Africans could not be considered property because their enslavement was illegal. The US attorney appealed the decision to the circuit court and later the Supreme Court on behalf of the Van Buren administration.

Attorney General Henry D. Gilpin argued that the captives were Spanish property based on the documentation aboard the Amistad and that they needed to be returned because of treaty obligations with Spain. Former President John Quincy Adams passionately defended the captives at the Supreme Court, and five days after Van Buren had left office, the court ruled in favor of the Africans.[51]

---

[51] Matthew Costello, "The Enslaved Households of President Martin Van Buren," *The White House Historical Association*, https://www.whitehousehistory.org/the-enslaved-households-of-martin-van-buren.

The Office of the Historian Archives reveals that former President and Secretary of State John Quincy Adams made a personal sacrifice to represent the Amistad Africans. An abbreviated version of his personal sacrifice and the subsequent Supreme Court's decision is as follows:

> To argue against the US Government for the Africans' freedom, the Christian Missionary Association convinced former President and Secretary of State John Quincy Adams to come out of retirement and face the predominantly Southern Supreme Court bench. In a masterpiece of American law, Adams presented the case of the Africans' freedom as a test of the American republic's sincerity in the ideals it espoused abroad. The Supreme Court ruled for the Africans, accepting the argument that they were never citizens of Spain and were illegally taken from Africa, where they lived in a state of freedom. The court acknowledged that the United States' argument that it had obligations to Spain under the treaty but said that the treaty "never could have been intended to take away the equal rights of [the Africans]."[52]

It is understandable how the former President and Secretary of State John Quincy Adams could masterfully defend the Amistad Africans when he is credited with expressing at the same time his artful defense the following: "Courage and perseverance have a magical talisman, before which difficulties disappear, and obstacles vanish into the air. Always vote for principle, though you may vote alone. If your actions inspire others to dream more, learn more, do more and become more, you are a leader." To forbid this chapter in American history from being used as a training tool to achieve a definitive step toward unification of

---

[52] "The Amistad Case, 1839," *Office of the Historian*, https://history.state.gov/milestones/1830-1860/amistad.

the American populace is to squash former renowned writer, humorist, journalist, and playwright James Grover Thurber's visionary words: "Let us not go back in anger or forward in fear, but around in awareness."

Additionally, to dismiss this chapter in American history that clearly justifies a reason for further discussions surrounding civil rights and social justice is to intentionally forget the past with the intention of repeating its horrific injustices and assaults on human dignity. To keep open the door for societal ills to dominate this system of living motivated by the abuse of power, authority, and prominence is to continue validating intellectual, emotional, and spiritual impoverishment. The Amistad story is an important narrative for this nation and the global community to honor because it captures universal arguments that support personal freedom and its interplay with unbiased justice. The Amistad narrative also highlights the sensitive balance between law, politics, and the ethical struggle. Recognition of a person's inherent credibility separate from economic, gender, race, ethnicity, religion, and age classifications creates the opposite of a deeply divided and fragmented society: a unified populace.

With certainty, censorship of this specific chapter in American history would deny the modern-day populace an example when credibility, relevance, and value were not solely associated with power, authority, and prominence. Long overdue are ethical examples for the American populace to experience when a former president and secretary of state and its judicial system, including the Supreme Court, are working simultaneously with one another to protect an individual's liberty and equality. During the time of the Amistad case, these branches of government recognized a valid legitimacy with respect to a person's inherent credibility, which was the linkage between genuine credibility, relevance, and value. Rather than the Africans being primarily viewed as free and autonomous individuals tending to daily affairs in their sovereign land, they were primarily associated with an external status, such as property and race, before being violently abducted.

The line of reasoning for preserving the Amistad narrative as a valuable segment of American history is revealed sixteen years later. The act of unification witnessed on March 9, 1841, was negated by the use of obnoxious power, authority, and prominence. Intellectual, emotional, and spiritual impoverishment made its hostile presence and strongly rejected the recognition of an individual's inherent legitimacy. The measure of healing that earlier was shepherded onto a divided American populace abruptly disappeared. The astonishing and shocking development in American history occurred on March 6, 1857, with the Supreme Court's decision regarding the Dred Scott v. Sandford case (John Sandford was, at the time, Scott's owner).

> The majority opinion of the Court, which stated that enslaved people were not citizens of the United States and, therefore, could not expect any protection from the federal government or the courts. The opinion also stated that Congress had no authority to ban slavery from a federal territory. This decision moved the nation a step closer to the Civil War. Though considered by legal scholars to be the worst ever rendered by the Supreme Court, it was overturned by the thirteenth and fourteenth amendments to the Constitution, which abolished slavery and declared all persons born in the United States to be citizens of the United States.[53]

According to Yale University's Yale MacMillan Center:

> Prior to the Dred Scott decision, the Amistad case was, arguably, the single most important legal case involving slavery during the nineteenth century. The Amistad case raised critical issues of law and justice. The central issue raised by the case was whether enslaved people had

---

[53] "Dred Scott v. Sandford," *National Archives*, https://www.archives.gov/milestone-documents/dred-scott-v-sandford.

the right to rise up against their captors in rebellion. Do people who are held illegally have a right to self-defense?

By 1839, the abolitionists had failed in their efforts to end slavery through moral suasion. Desperately, abolitionists sought a way to dramatize the horrors of slavery. The Amistad case seemed to provide a providential opportunity to illustrate the federal government's complicity with slavery and the discrepancy between slavery and American ideals of natural rights. The affair played a pivotal role in shifting the abolitionist movement away from the tactics of moral suasion to new methods of political and legal agitation, which would arouse substantial numbers of Northerners against the immoralities of slavery.[54]

The line of reasoning to preserve the Amistad story as an example of what unification looks like is further substantiated by the American Civil War, which began on April 12, 1861, and concluded on May 26, 1865. Four years after the alarming Supreme Court Dred Scott v. John Sandford decision, Americans entered into an agreement to go to war against one another. The condition of impoverishment struck an unparalleled low for both sides of the conflict. Destitution of thought was able to manipulate the estimated deaths of, roughly speaking, 360,222 Union soldiers and 258,000 Confederate soldiers. To this day, there remain scholars and historians who feel the actual death total is higher. Even so, completely lost on both sides of the conflict was a desire to value and protect an individual's inherent legitimacy through the art of negotiation, be it Union, Confederate, or slave.[55]

---

[54] "Document Essay: 'The Amistad Affair,'" https://glc.yale.edu/document-essay-amistad-affair.

[55] Bob Zeller, "How Many Died in the American Civil War?" *History.com*, August 23, 2023, https://www.history.com/news/american-civil-war-deaths

As a consequence of not being able to breathe life into the Declaration's claim—that all men (women) are created equal and are endowed with certain unalienable rights, including life, liberty and the pursuit of happiness—618,222 human beings, and possibly more, tragically lost their lives solely based on an ignorance of *unalienable rights*. It is true if an individual cannot identify, develop, and practice their inherent credibility as exemplified through attributes such as community, equality, compassion, integrity, transparency, fairness, respect, accountability, trustworthiness, authenticity, and responsibility, it will be an impossibility to breathe life into "We hold these truths to be self-evident."

The important theme surfacing from the Amistad narrative was the universal argument that supported personal freedom and its relationship with justice. Recognition of an individual's inherent credibility separate from external classifications—for instance, economic status, gender, race, ethnicity, religion, and age—created a unified populace. Regrettably, the American Civil War era had absolutely nothing to do with any mentality outside of satisfying self-important and self-indulgent agendas.

The central focus of the conflict for the South was directed at using power, authority, and prominence to achieve states' rights that would preserve their political control and an economic system primarily based on agriculture, with a heavy reliance on slave labor. The central focus of the conflict for the North was to continue expanding the federal government's authority over territories, which included the Southern states, develop a highly effective industrialized nation, a more unified economy and political system, and abolish slavery.

The line of reasoning to preserve the Amistad story reaches its pinnacle roughly two years into the American Civil War. The National Archives offers this explanation:

President Abraham Lincoln issued the Emancipation Proclamation on January 1, 1863, announcing, "that all persons held as slaves" within the rebellious areas "are, and henceforward shall be free." Even though sectional conflicts over slavery had been a major cause of the war, ending slavery was not a goal of the war. The Proclamation had the effect of changing the legal status of more than 3.5 million enslaved African Americans in the secessionist Confederate states from enslaved to free. Because it was a military measure, the Emancipation Proclamation was limited in many ways. It applied only to states that had seceded from the Union, leaving slavery untouched in the loyal border states.

In rebellion against the United States, the following, to wit: Arkansas, Texas, Louisiana (except the Parishes of St. Bernard, Plaquemines, Jefferson, St. John, St. Charles, St. James Ascension, Assumption, Terrebonne, Lafourche, St. Mary, St. Martin, and Orleans, including the City of New Orleans), Mississippi, Alabama, Florida, Georgia, South Carolina, North Carolina, and Virginia, (except the forty-eight counties designated as West Virginia, and also the counties of Berkley, Accomac, Northampton, Elizabeth City, York, Princess Ann, and Norfolk, including the cities of Norfolk and Portsmouth), and which excepted parts, are for the present, left precisely as if this proclamation were not issued.[56]

There is a compelling sentence on the third line in paragraph one. It reads: "Even though sectional conflicts over slavery had been a major cause of the war, ending slavery was not a goal of the war." This is an

[56] "Emancipation Proclamation (1863)," *National Archives*, https://www.archives.gov/milestone-documents/emancipation-proclamation.

educated guess in response to the statement. Had President Lincoln been more historically astute with respect to how the Amistad narrative became a societal and international success, he probably would have second-guessed himself. A decision not to release more than 3.5 million enslaved African Americans onto a landscape ill-prepared to encounter an enclave of people just out of bondage would have been a more prudent decision. However, the one-dimensional, short-term goal to break the fighting spirits of rebellious states was a military success. The focus was to bring to an end the more important internal war that was severely jeopardizing the attempt to externally unify this nation. For that matter, racism, with its subdivisions of discrimination, prejudice, and injustice, was already a deadly practice in the North.

According to APM Reports, *Shackled Legacy: Universities and the Slave Trade*:

> Profits from slavery and related industries helped fund some of the most prestigious schools in the Northeast, including Harvard, Columbia, Princeton and Yale. And in many southern states—including the University of Virginia—enslaved people built college campuses and served faculty and students. "The story of the American college is largely the story of the rise of the slave economy in the Atlantic world," says Craig Steven Wilder, a historian at MIT and author of *Ebony and Ivy: Race, Slavery, and the Troubled History of America's Universities.*

> Early benefactors who gave money to Brown and Harvard, for instance, made their fortunes running slave ships to Africa and milling cotton from plantations in the American South. Georgetown could afford to offer free tuition to its earliest students by virtue of the unpaid labor of Jesuit-owned slaves on plantations in Maryland. At the University of Virginia—founded

and designed by Thomas Jefferson—slaves cooked and cleaned for the sons of the Southern gentry.

"Yale inherited a small slave plantation in Rhode Island that it used to fund its first graduate programs and its first scholarships," Wilder says. "It aggressively sought out opportunities to benefit from the slave economies of New England and the broader Atlantic world." To date, there is no single accounting of how much money flowed from the slave economy into coffers of American higher education. But Wilder says most American colleges founded before the Civil War relied on money derived from slavery.[57]

In the end, using more than 3.5 million enslaved African Americans as pawns in a highly crafted strategic move to negatively impact Southern rebellious states was a no-brainer. Sadly, President Lincoln did not have a John Quincy Adams, a disturbed international community, a politically savvy, well-organized Northern Abolitionists group, nor a judicial branch of the United States Government, which included lower courts and the Supreme Court to loudly lobby: "Always vote for principle, though you may vote alone." The petition would also include thoughtfully contemplating the recognition that an individual's inherent credibility is separate from economic, gender, race, ethnicity, religion, and age classifications. Sadly, President Lincoln simply did not have time on his side nor a receptive environment, as did the Amistad narrative.

For a more comprehensive discussion regarding the American Civil War, refer to this author's 2023 release of the book *Trust the Confession: Disavow Ignorance for Personal Freedom.*

Because President Lincoln was recognized and known as an individual who possessed attributes of substantive character, such as honesty,

---

[57] Stephen Smith and Kate Ellis, "Shackled Legacy," *APMreports*, September 4, 2017, https://www.apmreports.org/episode/2017/09/04/shackled-legacy

humility, courage, grace, and resilience, he was given the benefit of the doubt. Had President Lincoln been more historically astute regarding the societal and international successes of the Amistad narrative, more time on his side, and at least a moderately receptive environment, he surely would have understood the importance of achieving both internal and external unification for the nation. Lincoln would understand that an effective way to challenge institutions of slavery in the South and institutions of discrimination in the North would have been to emulate, as much as possible, the Amistad narrative.

Due diligence would have required President Lincoln to take reasonable steps to prepare both Southern and Northern landscapes to first recognize their own inherent credulity, which is separate from external classifications. Lincoln would have saturated both landscapes with arguments that speak to the recognition of an individual's inherent credibility and its attributes of substantive character. For that reason—*who* President Abraham Lincoln was as a person—he would have created a unified populace in support of personal freedom, and its interplay with unbiased justice had he more time on his side.[58]

This nation is positioned at the same precipice that just under four million enslaved African Americans were positioned when President Abraham Lincoln signed into law the Emancipation Proclamation on January 1, 1863. However, instead of roughly four million Americans standing very close to the edge of a cliff and dangerous situation. There are approximately 333 million (2022) Americans. By January 1, 1863, millions of African Americans had fully learned what propelled this nation's system of living. They had learned how credibility, relevance, and value were primarily determined by the powerful, authoritative, and prominent. Currently, over 333 million Americans have learned and are learning the same lesson. The refusal to educate this populace to know that stable and authentic credibility, relevance, and value are

---

[58] "Abraham Lincoln Character Qualities," *Lincoln Heritage Museum*, https://museum. lincolncollege.edu/discover/alccd/profile/abraham-lincoln-character-qualities.

based on an individual's inherent legitimacy comprised of attributes that represent substantive character has moved this nation closer to the precipice of an internally self-inflicted collapse.

The contradiction between the principles of liberty and equality promoted in the Declaration of Independence and the existence of self-importance and self-indulgence was apparent in 1863, and it is apparent in 2024. An obsession with self-importance and self-indulgence is ultimately stimulated by intellectual, emotional, and spiritual impoverishment. The banning and censorship of reliable books that disclose this nation's societal ills and abuse demonstrative of this impoverishment position an uninterrupted path for the continuance of distorted credibility, relevance, and value. Linked with the cruelty attached to power, authority, and prominence, this nation's deeply divided and fragmented society can only continue to devour its own. On the other hand, working together as Americans to achieve unification of this nation is as the First Lady, Abigail Adams and wife to the second US President John Adams, states: "Great difficulties may be surmounted by patience and perseverance."

Chapter 5

THE CHOICE: TO LIVE OR TO SURVIVE

The one who plants trees, knowing that he will never sit in their shade, has at least started to understand the meaning of life.

—Rabindranath Tagore

The millions are awake enough for physical labor; but only one in a million is awake enough for effective intellectual exertion, only one in a hundred million to a poetic or divine life. To be awake is to be alive.

—Henry David Thoreau

As mentioned in Chapter Four, during the early stages of American history, numerous events exemplified acts of unification akin to the feats illustrated in the Amistad story. As previously noted, the individuals involved in the outcome of the Amistad narrative had to transition from a "will-to-survive" ideology to a "will-to-live" ideology to achieve unification. This transition was crucial to saving the lives of fifty-three Africans from the horrors of bondage and death and returning them to their homeland. The conclusion of the Amistad story highlights a profound realization: When the "will-to-live" ideology is bolstered by a conviction to recognize, value, and protect inherent credibility and its substantive qualities, it transcends the glorification or demonization of race, ethnicity, nationality, or gender. In essence, it prioritizes who an individual is internally and authentically over their external attributes or material possessions.

Surveying the early American racial landscape, countless acts of unification arose as a voice of disapproval against the misperception of racial superiority. American history reveals individuals who, despite being victimized by this ideology, committed themselves to reversing its destructive effects. Exceptional courage, resilience, and leadership characterized those who rejected the "will-to-survive" ideology in favor of personifying the "will-to-live" ideology. Their narratives have been documented, celebrated, and stand as enduring symbols of this transformation. Figures like Harriet Tubman, Frederick Douglass, Sojourner Truth, Nat Turner, Dred Scott, Crispus Attucks, and Ida B. Wells epitomize this principle. These individuals, often in collaboration with allies from diverse socioeconomic backgrounds, embodied the spirit of unification.

Among the many narratives from early American history that underscore unification, one stands out for its profound triumph over an impoverished way of life—a life sustained by laws that upheld the institution of slavery. This narrative focuses on Michael Morris Healy, Eliza Clark Healy, and their children. Michael Healy, arriving in America from Ireland at the age of twenty-two, initially epitomized the "will-to-survive" ideology. Preoccupied with self-importance and self-indulgence, his early focus was on accumulating wealth, power, and prominence.

A Shift from the Will to Survive to the Will to Live

However, Michael Healy faced a critical turning point. Confronted with the potential loss of Eliza Clark Healy, a sixteen-year-old enslaved woman he eventually took as his common-law wife, and the potential bondage of his children, Healy's perspective began to shift. He transitioned from a "will-to-survive" ideology to incorporating the "will-to-live" ideology into his life. Attributes like empathy, humility, ingenuity, integrity, and compassion began to shape his decisions, guiding him to protect the inherent credibility of his immediate family. No longer could he blindly accept the intellectual, emotional, and spiritual impoverishment of racial superiority. Healy was on the verge of a transformative realization, aligning with the sentiment of Dr. Maya Angelou's famous words: "If you're always trying to be normal, you will never know how amazing you can be.[59] Be a rainbow in someone else's cloud."[60]

This transformation, however, was not immediate. Until his departure from Georgia to move north, Healy clung to his "will to survive" mindset by continuing to own slaves, equating this with wealth and societal status. It was only shortly before his death that Michael Healy fully embraced the "will-to-live" ideology and disavowed the "will-to-survive" ideology. He came to understand that while nature determined his identity as a white male, his capacity for unconditional love and integrity defined his humanity.

James M. O'Toole, Associate Professor of History at Boston College and author of *Passing for White: Race, Religion, and the Healy Family, 1820–1920*, skillfully captures the Healy family's remarkable journey. Lois E. Horton and James Oliver Horton, authors of *In Hope of Liberty and Black Bostonians*, describe O'Toole's narrative proficiently on his book's back cover:

> O'Toole tells the remarkably well-documented story of an American family negotiating the terrain of race and ethnicity in the nineteenth century. Working at the intersection of church history and racial and ethnic

---

[59] Maya Angelou, *Rainbow in the Cloud: The Wisdom and Spirit of Maya Angelou* (New York: Random House, 2014), 84.

[60] Maya Angelou, *Letter to My Daughter* (New York: Random House, 2008), xxi.

history, he demonstrates that racial categories have been more fluid than law and custom admit. The Healys found freedom and extraordinary achievement by embracing their Irish heritage and the Catholic faith while distancing themselves from their African roots and slave status. This important book presents a more complex American racial past and contributes to our understanding of the challenges of a multiracial future.[61]

A Story that Was Buried but Needed to Be Told

In O'Toole's prologue, he reminds readers that the story of Michael Morris Healy and Eliza Clark Healy could not be divulged or revealed on a national level for at least two generations, up to the mid-1950s. For example, Michael and Eliza's granddaughter, Bessie Cunningham, living in Boston, and her cousin, residing in Santa Barbara, California, both resisted attempts by Jesuit priest and historian Albert Foley to investigate and publicize his findings. O'Toole writes: "Michael and Eliza Healy had been dead for more than a century, but to Mrs. Cunningham, they were still dangerous." She says to Foley, "I can see no reason for delving back over a hundred years. The inevitable result would be to make my children and their children very unhappy. What good will it do to anyone now? We cannot go back a hundred years to right things, and it surely is not our fault that such things should have happened to our family."[62]

In response to the grandchildren's panic, two questions arise. At least two generations removed from the original cast of characters, what was the secret that sickened the grandchildren and other family members? Secondly, what was Mrs. Cunningham referring to when she

---

[61] James M. O'Toole, *Passing for White: Race, Religion, and the Healy Family, 1820–1920* (Amherst, MA: University of Massachusetts Press, 2002).

[62] O'Toole, *Passing*, 1.

stated, "It surely is not our fault that such things should have happened to our family"? As it turns out, Foley was not the first scholar turned aside and told to leave bygones in the past. A graduate student preparing to study the Healy family had also been told to choose another topic by a senior professor aware of the family secret. However, life teaches us that the truth eventually prevails, and in time, the family secrets were revealed.

In 1954, Albert Foley, after ignoring years of appeals from Healy descendants to leave the family alone, published his biography of Michael and Eliza Healy's oldest son. The family secret was finally exposed. The roots of this mystery can be traced back to 1829 when Michael Healy, an Irish immigrant, and Eliza, an African American slave, lived together faithfully as husband and wife until their deaths within a few months of each other in 1850. O'Toole reminds readers: "In so doing, they violated perhaps the most powerful taboo of nineteenth-century America: marriage between persons of different races. Horror at this prospect arose from the understanding of what race itself was. For people of their time, the word had a clear, even scientific, definition: race depended on blood."[63]

O'Toole provides perspective to better grasp the need for secrecy. He states:

> In the America of the 1950s, an America in which strict racial segregation was the law in many places and the custom in most, a revelation of this kind might indeed be shattering, especially to those who thought of themselves as situated unambiguously on the white side of the color line. To acknowledge that a forebear had been black was to risk reclassification of the subsequent generations. The taint—it was seen as a taint, a bad and 'sordid' thing—of 'black blood' was permanent

---

[63] O'Toole, *Passing*, 14.

and irreparable, and its effects were still potent long afterward. If Eliza Healy had been black, the thinking went, then so were her children, and their children, and all the rest of the family.[64]

Beginning with a Will to Survive

The events leading up to 1829 and those that followed Michael and Eliza Healy's marriage until their deaths are pivotal to understanding this narrative. Michael Morris Healy was born on September 29, 1796, in County Roscommon, Ireland. As a nineteen-year-old white male immigrant, he is believed—according to family legend—to have deserted the British Army in Nova Scotia during the War of 1812. By 1818, after arriving at the port of New York, Michael took the Oath of Allegiance to the United States at the Jones County Courthouse in Georgia.[65]

Invoking a "will-to-survive" mentality in search of personal meaning and purpose, he soon traveled south to Georgia. Named after King George II, Georgia had been colonized by Europeans eager to claim land previously belonging to the Cherokee, Creek, and other Native American tribes. The redistribution of this frontier land to settlers willing to clear and cultivate it for agricultural purposes became a key initiative. Crops like cotton, tobacco, rice, and sugarcane dominated the agricultural landscape.

Farmers willing to take on a labor-intensive endeavor to clear the land and primarily develop agricultural crops such as cotton, tobacco, rice, and sugarcane could participate in redistribution efforts. Here is when Michael Healy became more than a mere Irish immigrant in search of personal meaning and purpose. A customary practice for

---

[64] O'Toole, *Passing*, 4.

[65] Michael Morris Healy, *Find a Grave* Memorial No. 126543874, Healy Cemetery, Jones County, Georgia, USA, https://www.findagrave.com/memorial/126543874/%20 michael%20_morris_%20healy.

local commissioners occurred seven times in a five-year period. The commissioners would conduct a land lottery for parcels of two hundred acres each, in which free white males, widows with children, and minor orphans were eligible to take part. These individuals would place their names in one container and the numbers of the land lots in another container.

In the beginning, as good fortune would have it:

> Michael Healy's name was drawn in 1823, and he took two more parcels in the drawing of 1832. Eventually, he held 1,500 acres, 800 of them 'improved' and in use, 700 more 'unimproved and waiting for development or sale.' The land was assessed in 1850 at the impressive sum of $7,500, and that placed him near the top of the heap. The census that year listed 412 landowners in the county: in improved acreage, Healy ranked thirty-third; in total land value, he was thirty-sixth. Though the land he was awarded was in a different location, he was able to eventually conduct transfers of lands with other farmers. Wealth in the Antebellum South was measured not only in land and liquid assets but also in slaves. Here, too, Michael Healy stood out.
>
> In 1830, the federal census reported that he owned thirteen slaves—seven men and six women—a respectable number for the time. Over the next twenty years, however, his slave ownership grew just as impressively as the rest of his property. By 1850, he owned forty-nine slaves, well above the local average of fourteen; of nearly 500 slaveowners in Jones County, he ranked eighteenth. Healy's slaves were estimated to be worth $22,000, but

when they were finally sold, they brought in almost $34,000, a staggering sum for the time.[66]

It was important to choose a crop among cotton, tobacco, rice, and sugarcane in the Macon, Georgia, topography that would return a reliable flow of cash, and cotton became that destinated crop or agricultural "king." Eli Whitney's invention of the cotton gin in 1793 helped Georgia farmers who were supplying cotton to the mills of Old and New England experience limitless demand. Prosperity for Michael Healy with his initial thirteen and subsequent forty-nine slaves was no stranger. On the surface, execution of the will-to-survive ideology through attainment of power, authority, and prominence had proven a huge success. Referred to by the neighboring community as the Healy Plantation, his home included a three-room farmhouse, adjacent barns, slave's quarters, animals, fourteen horses, forty milk cows and cattle, approximately 100 hogs, and a few random chickens.[67]

Inside the farmhouse, Healy had accumulated the material evidence of every imaginal comfort power, authority, and prominence that could stockpile to substantiate credibility, relevance, and value. Furniture for his bedroom and parlor, carpeting for the floors, wine glasses, a functional kitchen, "a handsome birdcage and a fiddle" were also external evidence of success. To further secure this legitimacy, Michael Healy had assembled an extensive library that amounted to over 100 volumes. His library included history, biography, philosophy, religious books, and medical texts. Reputable authors such as Lewis and Clark, David Hume, Shakespeare, Walter Scott, and Edward Gibbons helped to fill his bookshelves.[68]

Once again, on the surface, Michael Healy had proven his success by meeting and surpassing societal and cultural standards used to determine power, authority, and relevance. The only chapter of success

---

[66] O'Toole, *Passing*, 12.

[67] O'Toole, *Passing*, 13.

[68] O'Toole, *Passing*, 13.

THE ART OF UNIFICATION

missing from his personal portfolio was marriage and children. From his societal and cultural standing, it was clear Healy could have asked any woman of his race to exchange marriage vows and be a potential mother to the birth of his children. Instead, at the beginning of 1829, he chose Eliza Clark, a sixteen-year-old female slave, as his common-law wife.

Evidence of Healy's Shift in Ideology to the Will to Live

Pertinent information during this era regarding a slave's origins was considered irrelevant. Therefore, not much is known about Eliza, except her estimated birth date and the fact that Clark was her last name. This could suggest Eliza may have taken the last name of her former slave owner. What is also of interest is how later discoveries involving Eliza's classification describe her as "Mulatto." Again, during this era, this is the primary term used during the 1800s across the United States to classify individuals of mixed African and European ancestry. The term "Creole" was used for the same classification purpose but applied only to people who were born in and inhabitants within the Louisiana region.[69]

O'Toole's commentary:

> The decision Michael Healy made about marriage, however, was startling for his era, running contrary to some of his community's most deeply held beliefs and prejudices. In fact, he never legally married at all. Instead, he spent his life in a common-law marriage with a woman who was at once his wife and his slave. In so doing, they violated perhaps the most powerful taboo of nineteenth-century America: marriage between persons of different races. Horror at this prospect arose from the understanding of what race itself was. For people of their time, the word had a clear, even scientific,

---

[69] O'Toole, *Passing*, 14,15.

definition: race depended, literally, on blood. The content of one's veins determined who one was forever.[70]

Throughout the Antebellum South, early American history is detailed with how common it was for slaveowners to establish long-term
sexual unions with some of their slaves. To father children by them,
even as they maintained "respectable" marriages with white women, was
also a common practice. On the contrary, O'Toole suggests something
different in terms of commitment for one couple. He states:

> But neither Michael Morris Healy nor Eliza Clark Healy
> ever married anyone else; they lived together faithfully
> for twenty years until their deaths within a few months
> of each other in 1850. Even so, Michael Healy pub-
> licly acknowledged their connection, referring in his
> will, first drafted in 1845, to "my trusty woman Eliza,
> mother of my said children." The two were husband
> and wife in everything but law. Georgia law made it
> impossible for this marriage to ever be sanctioned by the
> state, and there is no evidence that they approached a
> clergyman to formalize it, something a priest or minis-
> ter would, in any event, have been forbidden by law to
> do. Nor could the owner grant his wife her freedom, for
> manumission had by then been restricted to exceptional
> cases and could be done.[71]

At this point, it becomes necessary to invoke the British writer
and physician Sir Arthur Conan Doyle's fictitious detective Sherlock
Holmes's application of deductive reasoning. To understand Michael
Healy's shift from a fixation with the will to survive and its focus on
power, authority, and prominence to embrace its opposite, the will to

---

[70] O'Toole, *Passing*, 14.

[71] O'Toole, *Passing*, 14, 17.

live and its focus on personal empowerment, necessitates reasoning backward. For Michael Healy to live faithfully with Eliza Clark Healy for twenty years until their deaths, publicly acknowledge their connection in his will during 1845, refer to her as "my trusty woman, mother of my children," and O'Toole to narrate the statement, "the two were husband and wife in everything but law" suggests a profound shift in Michael Healy's ideology. It is apparent that just prior to 1850, Healy had embraced the will to live, which was shown by attributes such as empathy, gratitude, compassion, mutuality, accountability, devotion, transparency, authenticity, and responsibility.

A Culture of White Supremacy in Nineteenth Century Academia

Reasoning backward to understand how Michael Healy came to this transition has to begin with O'Toole's statement regarding Healy's desertion from the British Army in Canada during the War of 1812 possibly being the creation of family legend. True or not, the will to survive the daily struggles of his modest and rustic experiences growing up in County Roscommon, Ireland, coupled with the cruel conditions and inflexibility of military life, would make sense as the sources for personal and political motivations, desertion or not. What conceivably may have pushed him over the edge to pursue a better life elsewhere was the possibility of having to endure the pervasive anti-Irish sentiment within the British ranks. The animosity between the two cultures was troublesome and well-known to exist.

An opening to fulfill self-importance and self-indulgence with the prospect of attaining land and personal freedom in the United States had to be a robust inducement. The opportunity to not only escape British rule but to achieve social and economic advancement based on an ethnicity that previously provided negative experiences must have felt personally overwhelming. Also, in the United States, Michael Morris

Healy would experience a substantial upgrade in his racial credibility and legitimacy.[72]

The upgrade of Michael Healy's racial credibility and relevance would begin as an after-effect of the third publication of *On the Natural Varieties of Mankind*. The acclaimed and prominent German physician, naturalist, and anthropologist Johann Friedrich Blumenbach initially released his racial bolt of lightning in 1795. In the United States, racial classifications were faithfully followed as a buttress to his work. By studying various human varieties based on physical characteristics such as skin color, skull, and facial features, Blumenbach established the term "race" to categorize different human populations. In succession, he ranked the different varieties in terms of importance and beauty. Blumenbach also established the term "Caucasian" to signify the white race, which applied to Europeans, Middle Easterners, and South Asians with the ranking of number one. Mongolian, Malayan, Ethiopian, and American races followed in that order.[73]

The seeming motivation to rank human varieties based on physical characteristics, which included beauty as a prime feature, clearly served one fundamental resolve. The jerry-rigged classifications with the white race ranked as number one put into play a will-to-survive dogma that established positions of power, authority, and prominence for the recently named Caucasian race. Unknowingly, Michael Healy would immediately benefit from Blumenbach's efforts, and his children would, in the future, also benefit from like-minded efforts that followed the German physician and anthropologist's initial proclamation. As the offspring of interracial parents, sons and daughters who could pass for

---

[72] Enya Holland, "Anti-Irish Sentiment in Early Modern Britian," *The York Historian*, June 17, 2017, https://theyorkhistorian. com /2017/06/22/anti-irish-sentiment-in-early-modern-britain/.

[73] Lorenzo Leonard, *Trust the Confession: Disavow Ignorance for Personal Freedom* (USA: Elevate Press, 2023), 178.

white as adults would be the recipients of a definitive form of legitimacy and superiority.

Moving to lend support and help advance Blumenbach's assertion of white race superiority were the like-minded efforts put forth by the French diplomat, writer, ethnologist, and social thinker Joseph Arthur de Gobineau. His treatise, *An Essay on the Inequality of Human Races* (1853–1855), proclaimed:

> The superiority of the white race over others and labeled the "Aryans"—i.e., the Germanic peoples—as representing the summit of civilization. He advanced the theory that the fate of civilizations is determined by racial composition, that white and, in particular, Aryan societies flourish as long as they remain free of black and yellow strains, and that the more a civilization's racial character is diluted through miscegenation, the more likely it is to lose its vitality and creativity and sink into corruption and immorality. Gobineau's theories, now discredited, were the product of years of historical, anthropological, and ethnological studies and were part of a general European interest in biological and sociological determinism.[74]

To support and help advance Gobineau's treatise was Houston Stewart Chamberlain's essay entitled *Foundations of the Nineteenth Century* (two volumes, 1911).[75] Chamberlain's dissertation represented a broad but biased analysis of European culture, in which he claimed that the Western Aryan peoples had been responsible for the greatness and creativity of Europe and that the Jewish influence had been primar-

---

[74] "Arthur de Gobineau," *Brittanica*, https://www.britannica.com/biography/Arthur-de-Gobineau.

[75] Houston Stewart Chamberlain, *Foundations of the Nineteenth Century, In Two Volumes* (London: John Lane Company, 1911).

ily negative. The Aryan race was responsible for all the major advances in human civilization and should be preserved from intermixing with other races. As stated, Chamberlain's theories owed much to the writings of Joseph Arthur de Gobineau, who was the first to claim to prove the superiority of the "Nordic" race.[76]

Well after Michael Healy's passing, more justification for the superiority of the Caucasian race was publicized. Within the first quarter of the twentieth century, the American lawyer, historian, and anthropologist Madison Grant argued in his book *The Passing of the Great Race* (1916) for the superiority of the Nordic race and was a strong advocate for eugenics and immigration restrictions in the United States.[77]

Bringing up the rear to solidify the white race's will-to-survive ideology midway through the twentieth century was the American physical anthropologist Carleton S. Coon with his thesis *The Origin of Races* (1962). "Coon maintained that the human species was divided into five races before it had evolved into Homo sapiens and that the races evolved into sapiens at different times. Coon's thesis was used by segregationists in the United States as proof that African Americans were 'junior' to white Americans and hence unfit for full participation in American society."[78]

The granddaughter, Bessie Cunningham, and her cousin residing in Santa Barbara, California, both believed strongly they had very good reasons to reject any connection to their grandparents, Michael and Eliza Healy. Their loyalty to the will-to-survive ideology and desire to escape societal condemnation outranked recognizing appreciation for

---

[76] "Houston Stewart Chamberlain," *Britannica*, last updated January 5, 2025, https://www.britannica.com/biography/Houston-Stewart-Chamberlain.

[77] "Excerpt from Madison Grant, The Passing of a Great Race (1916)," *Oxford Learning Link*, https://learninglink.oup.com/access/content/schaller-3e-dashboard-resources/document-excerpt-from-madison-grant-the-passing-of-great-race-1916.

[78] John P. Jackson, Jr., "In Ways Unacademical: The Reception of Carleton S. Coon's 'The Origin of the Races,'" *JSTOR* 34, No. 2 (Summer, 2001), pp. 247–285, https://www.jstor.org /stable/4331661.

their grandfather's choice to embrace the will to live. To personally live outside oppressive societal customs with authenticity and devotion to Eliza and their children was not an option to value. With the public domain being flooded with academic publications proclaiming white supremacy over other races of people and specifically denouncing with mockery African Americans, passing for white was more important for survival purposes. Even though Michael and Eliza Healy had been dead for more than a century, Mrs. Cunningham and her cousin felt, based on current societal racial standards, both were still too dangerous to acknowledge as past Black blood relations.

Fortunately, the past efforts of theorists and their ideas to champion the superiority of Caucasian, Aryan, and Nordic races over other races have been broadly discredited by modern science. To rank these races over an array of different global races based on intelligence, importance, and beauty is nothing more than self-importance and self-indulgence run amok. The lack of any scientific basis for race superiority is essentially nonexistent, and in its place, the community has come out in favor of fundamental parity among humans. The parity that is shared among the global community comprises the qualities that shape an individual's inherent credibility, an area even the scientific community could learn more about.

Dilemma: Pursue External Status or Develop Substantive Character

The practice of solely linking credibility and relevance based on the external status and beauty of a person or group of people continues to amplify the negative impact intellectual, emotional, and spiritual impoverishment has on society. With a focus on attaining legitimacy strictly through external means, abusive power, authority, and prominence dictate the practices of discrimination and injustice to achieve their goals. To acknowledge the substantive qualities of an individual's inherent credibility places humanity on an equal foundation, irrespective of external characteristics. It is apparent that Blumenbach's personal attachment to the will-to-survive ideology motivated him to devise his treatise. Blumenbach's state of impoverishment based racial credibility, relevance, and value on a ranking system with the white race (now referred to as Caucasian) placed as number one. This recognition also established the abusive use of power, authority, and prominence by this race to bolster its ranking. The act of unification was soundly defeated, generating societal fragmentation among the populace to be fought against down the road.

It is understandable what motivated Michael Healy to immigrate to America. The will to survive had to play a prominent role, which would include satisfying his physiological needs, personal safety and security, and his need to experience respect, recognition, purpose, and meaning. However, socioeconomic conditions established in America prior to his arrival were solely based on the power, authority, and prominence used to create cultural inequities and inequalities. These imbalances assisted and guaranteed his survival. Fast forward to his commended economic and social successes as a cotton farmer and landowner, paired with the decision he made in 1829 to make Eliza Clark his common-law wife. A common phenomenon can begin to preoccupy an individual once the will to survive has been self-professed as triumphant. It is not unusual for an individual, after enjoying a series of events that involved indulging oneself with all the material possessions and external successes made available, to eventually experience an emotional and intellectual deflation.

Self-satisfaction begins to gradually fade into the backdrop, giving way to an invasive uneasiness that evolves around an internal longing for authentic, honest, and substantive experiences, which include associations. The soul will always desire its natural habitat shared with the genuine, no matter how much the outer disguise may distort itself. The susceptibility to experiencing an internal emptiness that material resources and external successes simply fail to sufficiently distract a person from can be distressing. The pursuit of power, authority, and prominence, mostly through material resources and external successes, does not provide the latitude for authenticity to occur. Realistically speaking, how can authenticity plausibly exist when a culture is fixated on attaining material properties and external successes to achieve power, authority, and prominence for the purpose of establishing credibility, relevance, and value?

It is not improbable that Michael Healy, after achieving the height of material successes and his external status, arrived at a typical conclusion by means of thoughtful reflection. Being a person with ordinary emotional needs, he would ultimately make experiencing authentic, honest, and substantive relationships a priority in his life. It is also not implausible that Michael Healy understood, on an intellectual and emotional level, that choosing a woman to marry, to bear, and to help raise his children from his declared race of superiority, privilege, and entitlement could prove problematic. Living in a society that unfailingly adhered to the classification of races ranging from superior to inferior presented certain built-in drawbacks. For one, the woman he married from his own race would also believe in her superiority and entitlement because she was white. Two, it is reasonable to believe she would also embrace the will-to-survive ideology that focused on the attainment of power, authority, and prominence for the purpose of justifying her legitimacy.

Moving Beyond the Will to Survive in Relationship

Michael Healy had to confront a pivotal question: Would qualities such as humility, devotion, mutuality, compassion, adaptability, courage, tenacity, and self-discipline be possible in a marriage defined by the structures of superiority and entitlement? Of course, the initial relationship between Michael Healy and Eliza Clark began as one of master and servant, power and powerless. However, history shows that relationships, marriages, and romances throughout the global community—including those in this nation—often originate within formats rooted in inequity and inequality. In these early stages, dynamics of power often prevailed, bolstered by motivations like the need to establish credibility, relevance, and value; the desire to be loved; fear of loneliness; sex; financial incentives; or adherence to religious dogma.

Only when the pursuit of authentic, honest, and substantive affiliations become a priority can a relationship evolve beyond its initial framework of power and control. This evolution requires recognizing and valuing meaningful personal qualities as credible and relevant. Michael Healy could have married a woman from his own race, navigating issues of superiority and entitlement while relegating Eliza Clark to the status of a concubine. This was a common practice among many white slave owners. Such an arrangement would have significantly reduced the risk of retaliation from Georgia's officials and the local community. Yet Healy chose otherwise, likely because his relationship with Eliza Clark had transcended the master-slave dynamic, evolving into one defined by mutual recognition and respect.

Though personal information about Eliza Clark remains scarce—as a slave, she was largely absent from public record—the circumstances surrounding her transition into Michael Healy's home suggest that her personal qualities deeply influenced his decision. After consolidating his land and acquiring approximately forty-nine slaves to cultivate cotton, Healy seemed resolute in his choice to bring Eliza into his household as his common-law wife. It's reasonable to assert that over time, he observed qualities in her such as humility, devotion, mutuality, compassion, courage, adaptability, tenacity, and self-discipline—qualities that emerged as charismatic and credible to both of them. These attributes likely paved the way for their relationship to shift from one of power and control to one of reciprocity.

Healy's willingness to protect Eliza at all costs underscores this transformation. From the early stages of their relationship to the later years of their marriage, he demonstrated a profound commitment to her and their children. This commitment came with significant sacrifices, including the potential jeopardy of his reputation, her life, and the lives of their future children. Historian James O'Toole provides detailed information about the names and birthdates of Michael Healy and Eliza Clark's children:

> Eliza Clark Healy bore ten children with clockwork regularity, and, surprisingly enough, all but one of them survived the diseases of infancy and childhood. The oldest came at two-year intervals: James Augustine, born April 6, 1830; Hugh Clark, born April 16, 1832; Patrick Francis, born February 27, 1834; Alexander Sherwood, born January 24, 1836; Martha Ann, born March 9, 1838; Michael Augustine, born September 22, 1839. A baby named Eugene, born June 30, 1842, lived only a few weeks, but he was then followed by a second cluster of siblings: Amanda Josephine, born January 9, 1845; Eliza Dunamore, born December 23, 1846; and a second Eugene, born January 23, 1849.[79]

The Will to Live a Better Life for His Children

Living miles away from Macon, Georgia, and separated by a river, the Healy family's farm offered them some protection from the scrutiny of nearby neighbors. Michael's wealth and social standing further insulated the family, as success often commanded a level of deference. However, their situation was never entirely secure. Neighborly curiosity could quickly turn hostile when it came to the Healy's unconventional domestic arrangement. One such incident, detailed by O'Toole, "involved workers on the Ocmulgee flatboats stopping at the farm. After consuming homemade whiskey, one suggested that the Healy children

---

[79] O'Toole, *Passing*, 20.

would fetch a high price at the Macon slave auction. Michael Healy reacted swiftly and angrily, setting his dogs upon the intruders to chase them away."[80]

An article titled "The Provident Salvation of the Healy Children," published in *The Atlanta Constitution* on August 3, 1969, provides a slightly different account of the same event. Jack Spalding, the article's author, wrote:

> The seriousness of the situation was brought home to Mr. Healy one summer day. It was his custom to bring his children and meet his neighbors on the riverbank near the crossing of the Old Chehaw Indian trail. The river was narrow there, and the fishing was good. The planters and their families would spend easy days on the river fishing, in conversation, and social drinking. One day, one of the gathering pointed to the Healy children and remarked what a fine price they would bring on the Macon slave market. That was the end of Utopia for Mr. Healy.[81]

This moment was pivotal, marking the beginning of Healy's determination to extract his children from Georgia. Confronted with the North's disdain for miscegenation and the South's lethal enforcement of racial laws, Healy remained resolute. O'Toole elaborates:

> On the face of things—literally—white Americans generally supposed it possible to determine race just by looking but fears also persisted that this was not a precise enough test. As complexions multiplied, the ability of whites to identify the allegedly real racial essence

---

[80] O'Toole, *Passing*, 19–20

[81] Jack Spalding, "The Provident Salvation of the Healy Children," *The Atlanta Constitution*, August 3, 1969.

carried in the blood became more problematic. This only reinforced another fear: that some blacks could find a way to violate the American racial code, successfully pretending to be white instead of black. Dread of 'passing' was everywhere.[82]

The law deemed their mother a slave, and thus, their children were enslaved and illegitimate in the eyes of society. Michael Healy realized that the only viable solution was to move his children out of Georgia. Although racial attitudes in the North were also discriminatory, they offered the family a better chance for a less perilous existence. There, his children might even pass as white, escaping the harsh racial codes of the South.

From Oppression to Liberation through Education and Faith

Healy's substantial wealth enabled him to provide his children with an education and lifestyle befitting a prosperous family. Yet the challenge of relocating them undetected by local authorities and suspicious neighbors was immense. His willingness to shoulder this burden speaks volumes about the evolution of his character—from a man driven by survival to one guided by the will to live authentically and protect his family at any cost.

Once a year, Michael Healy would travel to New York or Boston to conduct his cotton business affairs. However, beginning in the early 1840s, Healy's trips took on a new purpose: searching for a means of escape for his children—and perhaps for himself and his wife as well. During these travels, Healy discovered an opportunity for his children's education through Quaker schools. In the metropolitan area of New York City, he found schools under the authority of the Quaker religious organization, a group that had taken a fervent stance against slavery. The *Society of Friends* viewed slavery as a contradiction to Scripture

---

[82] O'Toole, *Passing*, 21–22.

and the Christian message of equality, making them an ideal ally for Healy's plans. Consequently, he did not need to be overly concerned about inquiries into the background of his sons.

Around 1837, Healy enrolled his eldest son, James, then seven years old, in a Quaker elementary school in Flushing, Long Island. A year later, his second son, Hugh, joined James at the school, followed shortly by Patrick. James may have also spent time at another Quaker school in New Jersey. The prosperity Healy had achieved through his landholdings and agricultural success enabled him to remove his sons from the dangers of their home environment. Once enrolled, it was understood that the boys would not return to Georgia.[83]

Although Healy found success in securing his sons' education, the Quaker system had its limitations. The boys could only progress so far within the relatively small educational network. Yet fortune smiled on Michael Healy once more, mirroring the good luck he had experienced years earlier when he acquired two hundred acres of land in lotteries. In March 1844, during one of his periodic trips to the North, Healy met a fellow passenger on a steamer traveling between Washington and New York: John Bernard Fitzpatrick, a Roman Catholic priest who had recently been consecrated as the auxiliary Bishop of Boston.

The two men conversed at length during the voyage. Healy shared his concerns about the limitations of the Quaker schools and his desire to provide greater opportunities for his children. Fitzpatrick, enthusiastic about a new educational initiative by his church, suggested Holy Cross College in Worcester, Massachusetts. Founded to educate the sons of immigrants, the college offered a broader academic program, beginning with elementary education. Bishop Fitzpatrick's proposal was a revelation for Healy, as it provided an alternative pathway for his children's futures without probing their backgrounds.[84]

---

[83] O'Toole, *Passing*, 24.

[84] O'Toole, *Passing*, 25.

In 1844, James, then fourteen, was deemed sufficiently prepared by his Quaker education to enter the second year of Holy Cross's high school program. Hugh, age twelve, joined him in the same class, while Patrick, age ten, and Sherwood, age eight, were enrolled in the grammar school. Michael Healy's youngest son followed his brothers to Holy Cross in 1849. Upon their arrival, the boys were baptized by the Jesuits, marking a significant shift in their lives. Their education under the Catholic Church's guidance became a defining element of their identities.[85]

Martha Ann Healy, the eldest daughter, was the next to escape Georgia's racial confines. Following her brothers' enrollment, she was sent to Cambridge to live permanently with Eleanor and Thomas Boland, the sister and brother-in-law of Bishop Fitzpatrick. Baptized shortly after her brothers, Martha also became part of the small but vibrant world of Boston Catholicism. In 1848, during Christmas, the Healy brothers reunited with their sister at the Boland's' home, marking a pivotal moment of transition. The Catholic Church and its guardians had effectively become the children's new family, replacing the parents and siblings left behind in Georgia. (P.38)

Although Michael Healy had not actively practiced his Catholic faith for many years, Bishop Fitzpatrick's influence profoundly benefited his children and shaped the family's future. Through the Catholic denomination, most of the Healy children found their identities and life's work. By 1849, James graduated as valedictorian of Holy Cross's first graduating class, with his brothers Hugh, Patrick, and Sherwood also ranking at the top of their respective classes. Their academic success, coupled with Bishop Fitzpatrick's sponsorship, helped the Healy children navigate the challenges of being mixed-race in a predominantly white society. While their racial heritage was discernible to many, Bishop Fitzpatrick's support shielded them and facilitated their remarkable achievements.

---

[85] O'Toole, *Passing*, 28.

Jim Goulding, on March 10, 2014, posted a blog titled "The Healys: One Extraordinary Family." In it, he states:

> The four eldest Healy boys were high academic achievers. In 1849, James was the valedictorian of the first graduating class at Holy Cross. He ranked academically at the top of his class, and Hugh came out fourth. Patrick ranked first in his class and Sherwood was second in his. The fact that the boys did so well in their studies undoubtedly compensated in some way for the fact that they were mixed-race children in an all-white society. Also, their sponsorship by Bishop Fitzpatrick, who became head of the Boston diocese, went a long way toward gaining acceptance for them in what could be a clearly intolerant society. Others around them could fairly easily discern that they had Negro blood. In most of them, it was evident to a greater or lesser degree. But Fitzpatrick saw their potential, and he began grooming them for a higher calling.[86]

James, Sherwood, and Patrick would become priests, and all three of the daughters entered religious life in Montreal, Quebec, Canada. The oldest daughter, Martha, would leave the convent and marry a prosperous Irishman in Boston. James became the second Bishop of Portland, Maine; Patrick, a Jesuit, was the second President of Georgetown University, and Sherwood was appointed Professor of Moral Theology and Director of Student Discipline at St. Joseph's Provincial Seminary in Troy, New York. Sherwood's career in the priesthood was cut short by his death in 1875 at the age of thirty-nine. Amanda Josephine joined the Religious Hospitallers of Saint Joseph and would also die at age

---

[86] Jim Goulding, "The Healys: One Extraordinary Family," *The Wild Geese*, blog, March 10, 2014, https://thewildgeese.irish/profiles/blogs/the-healy-s-an-extraordinary-family.

thirty-nine. Eliza followed Martha into the Congregation of Notre Dame and went on to become a superior in the order.[87]

The Healy parents intended to sell their plantation and move to the North with their three youngest children. However, when the parents each died a month apart unexpectedly in 1850, their son Hugh Healy risked his freedom to return to Georgia from New York to take his three youngest siblings to the North. Still legally a slave in Georgia, he could have been captured by slave catchers and sold in the slave trade. After graduating from Holy Cross, Hugh Healy moved to New York City, where he was building a hardware business. As executors of his parents' estate, Hugh liquidated the plantation and other assets and returned to New York with his younger siblings. There, he arranged for them to be baptized as Catholics in the Church of St. Francis Xavier on June 13, 1851. Hugh Healy died at age twenty-one as a result of an infection contracted after a boating accident in the Hudson River.

In reflecting on the Healy family story, there are undeniable parallels to a Shakespearean play with respect to the narratives of Michael Morris Healy, Mary Eliza Healy, and their children. The Healy children's journey from the oppressive confines of Georgia to the liberating embrace of education and faith echoes the timeless struggles depicted in works like Hamlet, Romeo and Juliet, and Macbeth. These tales, like the Healys' own, are imbued with the dual forces of survival and a quest for meaningful existence. Their intermixed and separate stories are what have elevated Shakespeare's plays to the status of masterpieces that provide clarity to life's complexities.

For example, Hamlet, Romeo and Juliet, and Macbeth offer a mixture of darker themes, blissful endings, and historical events. For both Shakespeare and the Healys, this combination reflects the ever-present duel between the will-to-survive and will-to-live ideologies up to the

---

[87] "An Extraordinary Family: The Healys of Georgia," *Adrian Dominican Sisters*, May 13, 2022, https://adriandominicans.org/Equity-and-Inclusion/an-extraordinary-family-the-healys-of-georgia.

very end of their respective stories. Standing for the will-to-live ideology is the act of unification, which dances in and out of the Healy narratives in the same manner as power, authority, and prominence that stands for the will-to-survive ideology.

As this discussion pertains to Michael Morris Healy, it is sensible to assume that, as a young man growing up in Ireland, he was influenced by his homeland system of living. Generally speaking, Ireland was consistent with other global systems of living to the extent of embracing the well-known supposition to pursue material sources and external status as practical means to achieve personal power, authority, and prominence. The greater this accomplishment, the more esteemed an individual feels and credibility, relevance, and value are celebrated. Witnessing firsthand an Irish economy, mostly agricultural, economic hardships for farmers, limited industrial growth, and the social and economic disparities between rural and urban conditions can explain Healy's desire to immigrate to more promising economic opportunities in America.

However, Michael Morris Healy represents a classic example of what occurs for individuals who enter this life in possession of attributes that exemplify a personal value beyond what an individual is externally. As is the circumstance for many individuals entering this life, for Healy, there was a void within this system of living to help him recognize, develop, and demonstrate qualities that distinguished him as a person possessing principled character. Lacking this vital information, Healy was exposed to and influenced by a system of living and its ideology, which was the "will to survive." Upon his arrival outside of Macon, Georgia, Healy set out to pursue and achieve material sources and external status. In quick fashion, his personal sense of power, authority, and prominence elevated through the practices of division, strife, and the "chattel slavery" of African Americans.

Nevertheless, Michael Morris Healy came to realize the will to survive and its ideology in support of division were essentially unsatisfying and distasteful. This became more and more apparent to him as he developed compassion, commitment, and love for a live-in female slave who eventually became his partner in a marriage setting and the mother of their ten children. The will to live and acts of unification quickly replaced the system of living Healy was initially exposed to when arriving in America. Because he allowed his inherent attributes that characterized his principled character to dictate how he wanted to illustrate the will-to-live ideology, Healy was able to save his daughters and sons from falling victim to a will-to-survive way of life—this, before his partner and wife died just months apart from one another, as the plan was for them to also escape from the conditions of division and strife.

Chapter 6

THE WILL TO LIVE AND UNIFICATION

Love in its true form is an understanding and appreciation of what makes a person wholly unique. Love is really . . . a recognition of another person's integrity and truth.

—Robert Graves

To marginalize or obstruct efforts to inspire an individual or individuals to cultivate inherently bestowed qualities of substantive character unwisely nurtures one's own disenchanted and disillusioned soul.

—Anonymous

The best sermon ever preached is Truth practiced and demonstrated.[88] Behavior indicative of substantive character resonates more effectively than power, authority, and prominence when interacting with others. Essential to achieving this unpretentious empowerment and personal unification is a willingness to undergo

---

[88] Mary Baker Eddy, *Science and Health with Key to the Scriptures* (New Delhi, India: Namaskar Books), 201.

self-examination. "We cannot fill vessels already full; they must first be emptied."[89] This statement underscores the necessity of discarding selfish beliefs focused on attaining power, authority, and prominence. Such beliefs hinder the recognition of one's authentic credibility, relevance, and value. Suppressing the development of personal truth leads individuals into a competition for admiration dominated by narcissists. The egotistical pursuit of power, authority, and prominence attracts individuals preoccupied with themselves and their own needs, often fueled by deception and betrayal. These disingenuous practices have become habitual methods employed to gain socioeconomic advantages over others. Examples include access to better educational opportunities, securing high-paying job positions, gaining entry into exclusive social networks, accumulating wealth and real estate, or controlling resources and markets.

Discarding constricting self-misconceptions is essential for personal growth that encompasses authenticity. The statement that "we cannot fill vessels already full" emphasizes this by highlighting the need to abandon belief systems rooted in duplicity, seduction, and betrayal to achieve superficial credibility, relevance, and value. This way of life reflects the principles of a "will-to-survive" ideology, where the ends justify the means in the pursuit of power, authority, and prominence. Outside of self-serving intentions, this ideology disregards altruistic values. For instance, corporate profits often overshadow protecting the sanctity of individuals, democracy, as practiced, can serve as a historical cover for career politicians and aristocracy, and history is frequently sanitized to obscure unpleasant truths and exonerate the culpable. When the principles of the "will to survive" dominate, every facet of human life is negatively impacted.

By and large, relationships will be influenced by a sense of competition and self-preservation, which undermines developing trust and emotional intimacy. When personal survival is a key concern, passion

---

[89] Eddy, *Science and Health*, 201.

THE ART OF UNIFICATION

for equity and equality will diminish in terms of importance. Needless to say, unification on intellectual, virtuous, and emotional levels is lost. For example, relationships involving parenting and family interactions are reduced to task-focused endeavors. Survival-driven thinking generated by the will-to-survive ideology restricts the opportunity to nurture and be emotionally accessible. Outside of the home, the will-to-survive ideology undermines community and social bonds. Unification is not possible while individual survival remains a primary focus. And last but not least, a nationwide phenomenon, which is fitting with a persistent emphasis on survival, is the presence of anxiety, depression, and a diminished sense of purpose or self-actualization. The pursuit of power, authority, and prominence inspired by the use of seduction, deception, betrayal, and disingenuous practices fundamentally undercuts the possibility of community unification to exist.

In opposition to the "will to survive" is the "will to live." The opening to this chapter contains the following statements: "The best sermon ever preached is Truth practiced and demonstrated" and "We cannot fill vessels already full; they must first be emptied." Both statements are the creations of Mary Baker Eddy, an American religious leader who was the founder and leader of the Christian Science religion. As an author and teacher, Mrs. Eddy advocated for emotional, intellectual, and physical recoveries through principles that support the will-to-live ideology. The following principle supports this way of life: The best revelation an individual can be exposed to is the internal discourse that confirms the truth about oneself with respect to possessing inherent attributes that exemplify substantive character.

However, before this assertion can personally take place, an individual will need to empty their internal vessels. Personal values based on a belief system lacking a recognition and appreciation for inherent qualities limit the ability to avoid the development of a blemished and stained self-perception. Lacking this critical information lessens the opportunity to develop guardrails that protect an individual against developing disingenuous and deceptive behaviors. This personal deficiency substantiates the sentiment often attributed to Brazilian lyricist and novelist Paulo Coelho: "A mistake repeated more than once is a decision."

With this limitation, a person is compelled to adopt the will-to-survive ideology as a strategy to live their life. Power, authority, and prominence easily become personal goals to pursue. The disadvantage to using this strategy is the individual is left with one option to define himself, with self-perceptions primarily developed based on positive or negative experiences. Thus, the individual keeps his internal vessel filled with values that are morally weakened by an accumulation of personal misinformation that justifies disingenuous practices to achieve power, authority, and prominence. Experiences that commonly are positive inflate self-perception, and experiences that are, as a rule, negative deflate self-perception. Hence, the historically created superiority and inferiority of economic, religious, gender, racial, age, and physical differences are exploited as extensions of the will-to-survive strategy.

Mary Baker Eddy reaches back into history and discloses two distinguished examples that exemplify the "will to live." Both examples typified vessels first emptied that paved the way for the cultivation of inherently bestowed attributes that resulted in personal success based on substantive character benefiting the individuals and a receptive populace. Mrs. Eddy declares, "Mozart experienced more than he expressed. The rapture of his grandest symphonies was never fully heard. He was a musician beyond what the world knew."[90]

Wolfgang Amadeus Mozart confronted difficult challenges during his life. However, he refused to define himself by the experiences that would have diminished his inherent attributes and their value.

> Several difficulties appeared during Mozart's childhood
> despite his prodigious musical talents. One significant

---

[90] Eddy, *Science and Health*, 213.

challenge was the high expectations and pressures placed on him by his father, Leopold Mozart. Leopold was deeply committed to showcasing his son's talents to the world, which led to extensive and demanding tours across Europe when Mozart was very young. These tours, while providing exposure and opportunities, also meant a lack of stability and a conventional childhood for Mozart, as he was constantly traveling and performing. While Leopold sought fame and fortune through Mozart's talents, the family often struggled with financial stability. Even as an adult, Mozart faced money problems, partly due to irregular income and his extravagant lifestyle.

Additionally, Mozart's family life was marked by tragedy, as only he and his sister Maria Anna ("Nannerl") survived out of seven siblings. Mozart's extraordinary skill sparked envy among his peers and competitors. He faced challenges in gaining recognition and support from some members of the musical establishment, who resented his talent and sought to undermine him. During a tour in Paris in 1778, Mozart's mother, Anna Maria, died unexpectedly. This personal loss deeply affected him and marked a period of emotional hardship. These challenges shaped Mozart's character and career, but he persevered, leaving behind an unparalleled legacy of musical compositions.[91]

Mrs. Eddy goes on to state, "This was even more strikingly true of Beethoven, who was so long hopelessly deaf. Mental melodies and

---

[91] "Wolfgang Amadeus Mozart," *Encyclopedia Britannica*, https://www. britannica.com/ biography/Wolfgang-Amadeus-Mozart.

strains of sweetest music superseded conscious sound. Music is—the rhythm of head and heart in harmony."[92] As were the difficult circumstances facing Mozart, Beethoven also refused to define himself by his experiences that would have diminished his inherent attributes and their value.

> Ludwig van Beethoven faced numerous challenges during his childhood that profoundly shaped his life and music. Beethoven's father, Johann van Beethoven, was a strict and often abusive man. He was determined to turn Ludwig into a child prodigy like Mozart. Johann subjected young Beethoven to harsh and excessive musical training, sometimes waking him in the middle of the night to practice for hours.

> This caused immense emotional and physical stress. Johann was an alcoholic, which created instability in the household. His drinking habits strained the family's finances and left Beethoven with added responsibilities at a young age. The Beethoven family faced financial difficulties, especially as Johann's alcoholism worsened. This put pressure on young Ludwig to contribute to the family's income by playing music publicly and giving lessons.

> Beethoven experienced the death of several of his siblings during childhood, adding emotional strain to an already tumultuous life. Because of his family's financial struggles and his father's focus on his musical training, Beethoven received only a basic formal education. He struggled with spelling and arithmetic throughout his life. Beethoven had to take on adult responsibilities

---

[92] Eddy, *Science and Health*, 213.

early. By his teenage years, he was already managing household finances and caring for his younger brothers, particularly after his mother's death when he was sixteen. However, despite these challenges, Beethoven's early experiences likely fueled his resilience and passion for music, laying the foundation for his later genius.[93]

An earlier statement merits repetition due to its fundamental importance regarding living an individual's life free from adjusting to distorted self-perceptions: When negative or positive experiences impede the development and practice of attributes that exemplify a moral blueprint, the consequence for this neglect can be immense. Self-defeating choices and behavior, sometimes committed knowingly or unknowingly, can adversely impact an individual or group's intended plan or purpose. This particular consequence has been historically witnessed as a major cause for the collapse of societal institutions that precede the expiration of civilizations, dating back to the beginning of recorded history.

For example, history reveals government collapses due to corruption, authoritarianism, disregard for rule of law, and flawed economic policies. Religious institutions falter due to loss of credibility and relevance resulting from scandals, dogmatic inflexibility, or exploitation of followers. Educational systems collapse due to deficient funding, practices of inequality, and a failure to assist students in facing contemporary challenges that consequently lead to poor societal outcomes. Economies collapse due to unsound financial practices that promote inequity, inequality, and the exploitation of workers.

History also reveals societal institutions such as marriage and family eroding and collapsing when individuals or couples fail to prioritize mutual respect, communication, and effort. In addition, what has become a customary threat to family, generating separation or divorce of parents,

---

[93] "Ludwig van Beethoven," *Encyclopedia Britannica*, https://www.britannica.com/biography/Ludwig-van-Beethoven/Early-influences.

occurs when having children becomes a main focus before the couple has developed an emotional connection and mutual respect for one another. Due to this oversight, once the first or second child enters the relationship, one spouse feels alienated from the other. History is replete with examples of marital and romantic relationships collapsing when objectification becomes the primary reason or focus of the relationship.

Objectification reduces one partner to a set of characteristics—physical appearance, financial status, or social benefits—rather than valuing the other partner as a whole person with emotions, thoughts, and unique individuality. This search for an external source to provide the motivation to achieve power, authority, and prominence undermines the deeper, more meaningful aspects of a relationship. Without a moral blueprint affixed to the relationship, indispensable staples such as emotional connection, mutual respect, and shared goals will be lacking, and collapse is inevitable.

It is no secret—the longevity of any civilization will be determined by the duration its societal institutions can maintain and practice a truth that emanates from an established moral blueprint. Establishing this societal guardrail requires the implementation of an educational curriculum that helps an individual to identify, appreciate, and practice the best inherent qualities they have possessed since entering this life. Up through the twenty-first century, history has provided significant evidence to identify leading causes of the longevity of previous civilizations coming to an end. A primary reason for their collapse has been the failure to sustain commitments that adhere to a moral blueprint illustrative of the inherent value of each and every individual comprising its populace.

Civilizations such as the Sumerian Empire, Kingdom of Egypt, Roman Empire, Tang Dynasty, ancient Greek Empire, Byzantine Empire, French Monarchy, Tsardom of Russia, Kingdom of France

(Napoleonic Era), and Ottoman Empire all share common characteristics that led to their eventual downfall. The disintegration of infrastructures became unavoidable as they failed to sustain a commitment to advocate for a moral blueprint that recognized the inherent value of every individual. Self-interest, self-importance, and self-indulgence replaced a tattered moral blueprint. With a splintered society, social and civic deterioration, political and administrative corruption, economic and social inequalities, excessive taxation, and military overreach, the deficiency eclipsed the ability to reverse the ultimate collapse. The will-to-survive ideology weakened every infrastructure component as the pursuit of power, authority, and prominence became a compulsive pursuit. (For an expansive discussion regarding reasons for the inevitable collapse of previous civilizations, refer to Chapter 8 in the book *Trust the Confession: Disavow Ignorance for Personal Freedom,* published October 2023.)

Once more, "we cannot fill vessels already full; they must first be emptied." Avoiding the process of discovering one's own inherent rhythms of head and heart leaves an individual with only the "will-to-survive" ideology to embrace. Because this ideology has an enormous historical following, very little effort is put forth to resist its persuasion by the populace. As a result, this ideology easily becomes a dominant way of life to accept. With ease, the search for meaning and purpose becomes enthusiastic projections onto external sources for personal fulfillment. The pursuit of credibility, relevance, and value knows no boundaries or limitations. Symptoms that represent societal ills in the form of economic, gender, racial, ethnic, age, and religious inequities and inequalities represent the avoidance of discovering one's own inherent rhythms of head and heart.

The renowned English author Dame Agatha Mary Clarissa Christie, Lady Mallowan, is aware of this misguided effort and its consequences.

She used the idea that "old sins cast long shadows" extensively in her work and recognized their oppressive influence on a person's life will grow like a weed.[94] Enthusiastic projections attached to external sources for personal fulfillment can produce lasting aftereffects that are not always the desired overcome. The result of having chosen the will-to-survive ideology to live one's life in pursuit of credibility, relevance, and value through external sources can generate a crowded field of seekers with the same agenda. With this known fact, it is not surprising to discover how deception, disingenuousness, and betrayal are commonplace practices amongst this crowded field. Everyone in support of the will to survive is scratching and clawing their way to experience credibility, relevance, and value. The more power, authority, and prominence attained along the way, the more this fragile sense of self-fulfillment generates insecurity—hence, more need to create inequity and inequality across the board with respect to relationships.

When viewed as a personal failure to land amongst the formidable, who appear to be enjoying their positions of power, authority, and prominence, the toxicity can be consuming. This can resemble the morning after a dreadful night of drinking. The emotional, intellectual, and spiritual hangover due to internalizing this as a personal failure can affect an individual long after such experiences have passed. Disenchantment, disillusionment, and disappointment often creep into an individual's life for no other purpose than to inform the recipient of a sobering realization. When credibility, relevance, and value are mainly attached to external sources, it is wise to understand that external sources have definitive limitations.

The out-of-body and remote can never penetrate and satisfy the soul of its proprietor. Material wealth, race, ethnicity, career, marriage, romance, sex, physical beauty, relationships, religion, or child rearing will provide credibility, relevance, and value on a limited basis.

---

[94] Agatha Christie, *Elephants Can Remember* (Queensland, AU: Queensland Braille Writing Association, 1972), 64

Unfortunately, the pursuit of wisdom is the furthest inclination for an advocate of the will to survive. The disenchanted, disillusioned, and disappointed often double down with efforts to intensify their self-interest, self-importance, and self-indulgence. To continue the use of power, authority, and prominence as strategies to reach the status of the formidable and attain self-fulfillment parallels the predicament of the addict. But for a brief moment will the ecstasy last before more effort is deployed through the use of power, authority, and prominence to achieve the fragile hold of self-fulfillment.

"Old sins cast long shadows," and long shadows represent the serious consequences of avoiding the personal discovery and embrace of an individual's inherent rhythms of head and heart. So long as this discovery and embrace is prolonged, past experiences ending in disenchantment, disillusionment, and disappointment will continue to repeat themselves until the lessons they carry are fully learned. Values that impede the growth of our hearts and minds must be emptied of limitations and fear to be filled with the expansive understanding that recognizes an individual's inherent value and their unique rhythm of head and heart.

This sets the tone for a personal journey of introspection and transformation. Intellectual, emotional, and spiritual understanding emerge as one radiant discernment. This profound insight was brought to light by Martin Luther King Jr. and, with its engaging new data, briefly nudged attention away from *what* an individual is to *who* an individual is in terms of inherent credibility. Though the nudge may have been brief, this experience was also the catalyst for finally understanding the old saying, "The more things change, the more they remain the same."[95]

Socioeconomic reforms during the past century included social security and welfare systems to provide income for the elderly, disabled, and low-income individuals and families, including unemployed

---

[95] This proverb of French origin is often attributed to Jean-Baptiste Alphonse Karr (1808-1890). See Alphonse Karr, *Plus C'est la Même Chose* (Paris: Ancienne, Michel Lèvy Frères, 1876).

workers, children in need, and sometimes veterans. These programs aim to reduce poverty and provide financial stability for vulnerable populations. Out of necessity, the art of unification initially takes place on an individual level before it can be expected to occur beyond its borders. When the will to live has been adopted as a personal way of life, skills related to unification and community building become quite apparent The act to unify is demonstrated by behavior that recognizes credibility, relevance, and value inherently bestowed upon each and every individual. Disagreement and dissimilarities will certainly arise, but inherent credibility, relevance, and value relative to the individual will never be in jeopardy of denial. This personal initiative represents developed attitudes that go above and beyond the will to survive.

The will-to-live ideology represents conscious principled thinking that asserts personal development is established on unpretentious meaning, purpose, and fulfillment. This principled understanding endorses the recognition, cultivation, and practice of an individual's innate creditable attributes. The will to live is authenticated by exhibiting credible attributes such as integrity, honesty, compassion, fairness, courage, humility, community, perseverance, and empathy in one's life. Substantive character surfacing due to the acceptance of an individual's inherent credibility replaces a need to develop pretentious meaning, purpose, and fulfillment. The choice to live authentically will instinctively encourage unification with others and validate Friedrich Nietzsche's statement: "He who has a why to live for can bear almost any how."[96]

The following statement deserves repeating: When lacking personal information that confirms inherent qualities that exemplify substantive character, the lone option available to define oneself is predominately through experiences. To recognize and value the truth about oneself will always be the guardrail to protect against internalizing experiences that

---

[96] Victor Emil Frankl, *Man's Search for Meaning: An Introduction to Logotherapy, Fourth Edition* (Boston, Beacon Press, 1992), 109.

do not take into the narrative an individual's essence. The American writer Henry David Thoreau's words help a person from falling into false narratives: "Aim above morality. Be not simply good; be good for something."[97] Unfortunately, during the history of civilizations past and present, "he who has a why to live" has been minimized by strategies expressive of the will to survive. Propelled by intellectual, emotional, and spiritual impoverishment, the will-to-survive stratagems embody a lack of awareness with respect to an individual's core values as illustrative of admirable qualities. As a result of this deficiency, a person is deprived of an opportunity to experience what the renowned and popular Benedictine monk David Steindl-Rast describes: "Joy is that kind of happiness that does not depend on what happens."[98]

Thus far, throughout this chapter, the main focus has been on the individual and the importance of establishing unification on a personal basis. The focus will now shift to the importance of a civilization achieving unification amongst its populace to avoid a prevalent historical tendency to collapse. As previously discussed, the reason behind the collapse of previous civilizations has been due to a resistance to establish and adhere to a moral blueprint that represented all of its populace. It is true that before a civilization, nation, society, culture, or community can develop a moral blueprint committed to the will to live, this enterprise correctly first takes place on an individual level. An applicable format for this to occur is through an educational curriculum that teaches an individual to recognize, appreciate, and demonstrate the best inherent attributes they entered this life possessing.

An excellent example of the "will to live" during this modern era remains to be the United States Declaration of Independence, as brought forth by Congress on July 4, 1776.

---

[97] Henry David Thoreau, *Life Without Principle* (London: The Simple Life Press, 1905).
[98] David Steindl-Rast, *A Listening Heart: The Art of Contemplative Living* (Germany: Crossroad Publishing, 1983).

We hold these truths to be self-evident, that all men (women) are created equal, that they are endowed by their Creator with certain unalienable Rights, that among these are Life, Liberty, and the pursuit of Happiness. That to secure these rights, Governments are instituted among Men (Women), deriving their just powers from the consent of the governed. That whenever any Form of Government becomes destructive of these ends, it is the Right of the People to alter or to abolish it, and to institute a new Government, laying its foundation on such principles and organizing its powers in such form, as to them shall seem most likely to affect their Safety and Happiness.[99]

As stated at greater length in Chapter 4, when the *Declaration of Independence* was initially drafted by America's elite, the Founding Fathers, the intent was to use the document as a means to protect their privilege and entitlement, which included their wealth and accumulated power. This will-to-survive strategy also took into consideration avoiding British trade restrictions and taxes, preserving practices of gender inequality, upholding injustice and discrimination toward Native Americans and non-speaking Americans, as well as sustaining slave ownership of African Americans. The intention was obvious as the Founding Fathers and their landowning colleagues, during the beginning stages of America, held absolute power, authority, and prominence throughout the nation. It is important to note the will-to-survive ideology is a strategy designed to guard against efforts to unify a community, culture, and nation. To guarantee this intent necessitates that their power, authority, and prominence be protected at all costs.

The will-to-survive ideology—with an emphasis on attaining

---

[99] "Declaration of Independence," *National Archives,* https://www. archives.gov/founding-docs/declaration-transcript.

power, authority, and prominence—creates a distorted and often corrupt form of credibility, relevance, and value. Economic, gender, racial, ethnic, educational, healthcare, and age inequalities and inequities uphold imbalances and corruption. Unfortunately, from its early beginnings to contemporary times, the American way of life continues to be dominated by the will-to-survive ideology—and to inhumane degrees. This ideology's primary objective continues to be successful in turning Americans against Americans.

It is evident the will-to-survive ideology has a distinct mission, which is to encourage its supporters to seek and achieve supremacy over another person or group. The pursuit of power, authority, and prominence remains an achievable objective as long as credibility, relevance, and value are diminished to primitive, crude, and bottom-line perceptions. Consistent with this ideology is the lack of concern for dividing a populace and creating hostile divisions that are horribly frightening and life-threatening. Self-indulgence, self-interest, and self-importance remain cooperative bedfellows closely allied and connected to the will-to-survive ideology.

Conversely, it is true that during the past century significant socioeconomic reforms have taken place in America that have produced positive, yet limited, results. To a degree, increased numbers of Americans now considered themselves intellectually, psychologically, and emotionally entitled to be included and protected under the altruistic assertions of the Declaration of Independence. There were many social, political, and prominent activists leading the offensive to speak out against the intended exclusions. The anticipated hope that propelled the protest did lessen to measured degrees cruelties linked to the will-to-survive ideology. A semi-conscious shift to move in the direction toward a more unified society spearheaded by the will-to-live practice did come under thoughtful consideration.

The Declaration's decree regarding a person's inherent credibility, "endowed by their Creator," generated justified aspirations. Another source of welcomed inspiration came from the American Baptist minister, activist, political philosopher, and prominent leader during the civil rights era, Martin Luther King Jr. He introduced a new, different, and thought-provoking concept, which was the recognition of an individual's "content of character." In Martin Luther King Jr.'s "I Have a Dream" speech, delivered on August 28, 1963, during the March on Washington, DC, for Jobs and Freedom, he stated, "I have a dream that my four little children will one day live in a nation where they will not be judged by the color of their skin but by the content of their character."[100] This new concept of being judged by the "content of character" had never previously been discussed, at least not in open forums.

I could only assume, the thought must have crossed the minds of others, as it did for this writer, "What the hell is character?" I remember stating to myself, "No one has ever talked to me about character." Again, the assumption was made that Martin Luther King Jr.'s dream that one day in this nation, his children would be judged by the "content of their character" would become the dream for others, as it did for this writer. But just as important, if not more, King's dream became a catalyst to consider the meaning of character and its makeup. To be measured by personal attributes of genuine value that characterize who an individual is inherently—such as being a decent person, honest, attentive, reliable, empathetic, creative, industrious, accountable, and intelligent—was personally appealing. Moving beyond being judged based on economic status, gender, race, ethnicity, physical assets, religion, level of education, and age that characterized what a person is externally and possessed materially provided great emotional relief.

As a result of being impacted by Martin Luther King Jr.'s statement, another realization became apparent. This realization revealed the opportunity to respond differently to an old way of life devoted

---

[100] "'I Have a Dream' Speech," *History.com*, November 30, 2017, updated December 19, 2023, https://www.history.com/topics/black-history/i-have-a-dream-speech.

to the will-to-survive ideology. Instead of reacting with self-justifying, protective, and distrustful postures toward behavior seeking power, authority, and prominence at my expense, the answer was to respond with the will-to-live ideology as demonstrated by behavior. Memory had served me well, and this was how the Indian lawyer, anti-colonial nationalist, and political ethicist Mahatma Gandhi and Martin Luther King Jr. employed nonviolent resistance to the ferocious and threatening acts of violence exerted by power, authority, and prominence.

The will-to-survive ideology—upheld by individuals who strongly believe that power, authority, and prominence—is the bedrock for determining credibility, relevance, and value. The insight Martin Luther King Jr. emboldened his listeners with on the steps of the Lincoln Memorial in Washington, DC, was that power, authority, and prominence had nothing to do with credibility, relevance, and value. To the contrary, a person's substantive character illustrates their inherent value. Principled character embodies the best qualities a person enters this life in possession of, and it is a reality that represents legitimate credibility, relevance, and value.

Making yet another assumption, this, in part, may have been what Martin Luther King Jr. meant when he stated, "It doesn't matter now; I have been to the mountain top, and it is alright." Using inference, the mountain top could imply that he had experienced that eminent moment when the intellectual, emotional, and spiritual desires merged together: universal healthcare systems to ensure access to medical services regardless of income; fair labor standards and minimum wage laws; civil rights movements to terminate segregation and employment discrimination; women's rights and gender equality to tackle workplace equality, equal pay, reproductive rights, and discrimination; educational reforms to increase admission to public education and end school segregation; and environmental protection laws that created the US Clean

Air Act. It is a safe conjecture to accept that these and other unnamed reforms were brought forth with pseudo-good intentions.

From the beginning of this nation's inception to the present day, pursuing power, authority, and prominence has continued as its domineering way of life. And, as long as this will-to-survive ideology is a habitual way of life, socioeconomic reforms will continue to produce pedestrian and uninspired outcomes. Hence, pseudo-good intentions accompany each revision. Supporters of the will-to-survive philosophy will craft makeshift adjustments to give an appearance of compliance. For example, these makeshift adjustments can appear compliant while maintaining their independence. Supporters may use superficial documentation, such as posting official-looking signs or filling out paperwork without full adherence.

Minimum conformity allows these individuals to follow only the token requirements to avoid penalties while subtly resisting. Additionally, they employ alterable modifications, like temporary safety measures, which can be undone once scrutiny passes. This passivity will last until the backers of the will-to-survive ideology experience a favorable shift regarding the configuration of power relative to one or more branches of government: the executive, legislative, and judicial. And who are the supporters of the will to survive? The advocates are easy to detect—they are those who are steadfast in their belief that power, authority, and prominence are the pathways to achieve credibility and relevance.

Most conspicuous will be their steadfast need to control and dominate relationships. And just as obvious will be their rejection and refusal to support other individuals or groups who are also in pursuit of similar efforts germane to credibility and relevance. Again, the makeshift adjustments that give the appearance of compliance are energized by an incensed anger beneath the surface. This quasi-compliance will last until supporters of the will to survive experience a shift that favors their positions of power. This swing typically commences when political, civic, municipal, and judicial leadership represents the self-interest and self-importance of the will-to-survive enthusiasts.

With that having been said, lacking a practical moral blueprint for the populace to follow, rather than mere theoretical rhetoric, what is written in stone still prevails. A historically based Wild, Wild West approach to achieving credibility and relevance based on power and authority, in effect, turns Americans against Americans. Supporters of the will to survive make certain practices of inequality, inequity, and injustice remain in place by developing more and more sophisticated methods to overcome. Far too many career politicians, civic leaders, and judicial figures turn a blind eye to the shrewd and demoralizing strategies that keep this nation divided. For example, gerrymandering has been made a science by using advanced data analytics to lock in political control, silencing entire communities. Adding to this strategy, social media power brokers manipulate what we see through biased practices that amplify division and silence dissent. Adding to this division is the influence of dark money, which allows billionaires and special interest groups to effectively manipulate results behind closed doors while the public is left in the dark.

It is common knowledge that the justice system is not blind. Historically speaking, laws are selectively enforced to protect the will-to-survive powerful while disproportionately targeting marginalized groups. For example, racial and ethnic minorities often face higher rates of police surveillance, arrests, and harsher sentencing. Low-income individuals are more likely to be criminalized for minor infractions, while wealthier will-to-survive followers are afforded the opportunity to elude consequences for financial crimes.

There is a general consensus that immigrants and refugees entering this nation illegally has become out of control. However, rather than fixing the problem, these individuals are subjected to punitive enforcement, detention, and tactless deportation policies. Corporate media—owned by the same elites who fund politicians—twist narratives to serve their interests, creating echo chambers that deepen mistrust. Even voting, the foundation of democracy, is under attack through subtle suppression tactics like voter roll purges and reduced polling places. These practices don't make headlines because they operate in the shadows, but their impact is undeniable: they weaken trust, fuel division, and make true unity feel further out of reach.

Ironically speaking, the will-to-survive ideology that promotes the practice of division is supported by the increased numbers of Americans who now feel included and protected under the Declaration's altruistic ideals of equality, liberty, and justice. For example, women, racial and ethnic groups (African, Hispanics, Latinos, Native and Asian Americans), veterans, Americans with disabilities, the LGBTQ+ community, Dreamers (DACA recipients), and religious minorities (Jewish, Muslim, and Hindu) now consider themselves entitled to be legitimate pursuers of the Americans dream.

On paper, "the ideal that every citizen of the United States should have an equal opportunity to achieve success and prosperity through hard work, determination, and initiative" makes logical sense. However, both conscious and unconscious followers of the will-to-survive ideology have different agendas and other thoughts regarding what makes logical sense. The limited recognition attained by groups benefiting from socioeconomic reforms is based on what an individual is and does not take into consideration who an individual is, which adds fuel to an already burning fire with respect to turf wars.

A persistent challenge for Americans, whether new or old to the Declaration's inclusion package, is the failure to move beyond valuing individuals primarily by external identification and material possessions. With each reform introduced, a historic opportunity has been overlooked—one that could merge external recognition with a civic commitment to honoring substantive character. Unifying these aspects strengthens reforms, shielding them from the corruption that arises when power, authority, and prominence go unchecked. Without this civic foundation, division continues to overshadow unity. Elevating the nation's collective consciousness would have a lasting impact by fostering a moral blueprint grounded in practical action rather than theory.

Rather than allowing legitimate reforms to deteriorate under oppressive reactions, advocates for the will-to-live ideology can mount a counterattack. Those who believe power, authority, and prominence define credibility and relevance must be met with a proven response. Mahatma Gandhi and Martin Luther King Jr. provided humanity with such a strategy—nonviolent resistance. While there is no indication that the historically dominant will-to-survive ideology will fade, a foundational shift is required. To eclipse this mindset, the will-to-live ideology must be recognized and practiced on an individual level. Supporters can cultivate a personal way of life centered on the education and embodiment of character-driven values.

This approach prioritizes the recognition, development, and practice of inherent qualities such as authenticity, accountability, integrity, and community. Embracing a new ideology that unifies internal and external value is both daring and courageous. Followers of the will-to-survive ideology will offer seductive yet cruel distractions—ostracizing those who pursue personal empowerment instead of chasing power, authority, and prominence. Yet adopting the will-to-live ideology allows individuals to break free from the collective psychosis that compels people to compete for credibility, relevance, and value at the expense of others.

There is no question that external identification and achievements are important. However, when power, authority, and prominence become the primary markers of credibility and relevance, the consequences are clear—self-importance, indulgence, and entitlement dominate one's life. This obsession makes it difficult to see beyond oneself and recognize the worth of others. The relentless need to maintain credibility and relevance often leads to the abusive use of power, authority, and prominence, fueling systemic inequities—unequal school funding, healthcare disparities, biased hiring practices, unequal legal representation, and discriminatory lending. Likewise, inequality persists through gender pay gaps, racial wealth gaps, limited access to higher education, political underrepresentation, and housing discrimination. The old adage, "the more things change, the more they remain the same," holds true as reforms struggle to achieve lasting impact.

Tragically, the opportunity to apply the teachings of Gandhi and King in upholding the will-to-live ideology has quietly slipped away. Rather than elevating this nation to a more humane level of consciousness, America remains captivated by the theoretical language of the Declaration of Independence. The chance to counter the will-to-survive ideology with its antithesis—the will-to-live ideology—was lost. As power, authority, and prominence have become this nation's aphrodisiacs, so has the will to survive become more pervasive, which has rendered the will-to-live ideology a neglected way of life. Recognition, development, and practice of inherent character-driven qualities could have served as the unifying force for true inclusion, replacing a history of division.

This missed opportunity was swiftly seized by the technology industry—an ally of the will-to-survive ideology. Industry leaders and their followers, both reform beneficiaries and opponents, eagerly embraced the technological advances that further entrenched the pursuit of power, authority, and prominence. The industry's intended successes— enhanced connectivity, improved access to information, and increased productivity—are undeniable. However, the unintended consequences have deepened national divisions and intensified hostility.

If one were to take the pulse of the American populace today, the heartbeat would be racing—what will-to-survive advocates would call a victory. When people are constantly fed content that reinforces their existing beliefs and desires, it becomes increasingly difficult to see beyond themselves. The echo chambers of social media, the avoidance of discomfort, and the prioritization of convenience over community all contribute to a fragmented society. True unification requires shared experiences, empathy, and a willingness to look beyond personal gratification. But when technology fuels hyper-individualism, that journey becomes an uphill battle.

The art of unification of the American people is difficult to accomplish when the populace is consumed with its own self-interest, indulgence, and importance. Economic standing, political partisanship, profession, gender, race, ethnicity, religion, and age remain the basis for establishing credibility, relevance, and value. The misuse of power, authority, and prominence—to bolster what an individual is—remains vital for feeling credible, relevant, and of value. Currently, there simply is no mandate for Americans to change their hearts and minds by way of an educational curriculum that identifies attributes that comprise an individual's inherent credibility and the "content of one's character."

Transitioning from the will-to-survive ideology to a will-to-live way of life would also improve this society's chance to experience a legitimate sense of unification. This nation can move dramatically toward this goal by emphasizing the need to abandon belief systems rooted in duplicity, seduction, and betrayal to achieve superficial credibility, relevance, and value. The courageous act of emptying out the will-to-survive vessel and rebuilding a vessel exemplifying the will to live prolongs this nation's longevity as well. Such a dramatic shift in ideologies would exemplify Mary Baker Eddy's assertion that "the best sermon ever preached is Truth practiced and demonstrated." Once the altruistic claims of the Declaration of Independence are internalized, this nation will reach a level of purpose and validity never before experienced in its history: "for and by the people."

Chapter 7

FREEDOM AND DEMOCRACY OR NOT

Once you understand the power of your words, you
won't just say anything. Once you understand the
power of your thoughts, you won't just think anything.
And once you understand the power of your presence,
you won't just be anywhere. Know your worth.

—Anonymous

What I really need is to get clear about what I must
do, not what I must know . . . The crucial thing is
to find a truth which is truth for me, to find the
idea for which I am willing to live and die.

—Søren Kierkegaard

This chapter will not be reinforced with collaborating research, like-minded authors, or footnotes to support proclamations. Instead, it will primarily consist of this writer's adult observations and interpretations, shaped by personal experiences and the unfolding domestic events that have made one undeniable truth evident across this nation: The steady moral decline of long-standing institutions and the equivalent deterioration of American culture is no longer a matter of a figment of imagination or debate. It has become an undeniable reality. When self-interest, indulgence, and the pursuit of individual importance dominate a society to the extent we are currently witnessing, the results of such a state of affairs are both predictable and alarming.

From our nation's inception through its long and complex history, there has never been a clearly defined and domestically accepted moral blueprint to stabilize our society. While the Declaration of Independence contains theoretical ideals, and the phrase "American identity" induces a sense of national purpose, these words have long lacked a structured pathway to transform them into a lived and sustainable reality. The absence of this foundational moral guidance has left our nation vulnerable to moral decay. Is it any wonder that our domestic institutions and cultural landscape are in a state of moral decline? As a society, we have lacked the necessary training to recognize, cultivate, and apply the fundamental qualities that each American inherently possesses—qualities that, if developed, could provide substance and function to the principles outlined in the Declaration of Independence and the concept of the American identity.

This failure has allowed both the Declaration and the American identity to remain mere abstractions, oftentimes repeated but rarely realized. As a result, domestic leaders and various factions of the populace have resorted to the relentless pursuit of power, authority, and performance as a means of achieving superiority. This fragile and unstable pursuit has become synonymous with credibility, relevance, and value that must be protected at all costs. As a result, our institutions have failed to uphold the dignity and worth of all people, leading our nation further into moral descent.

For this writer, the time has arrived to bestow genuine meaning to the words that so many of our ancestors and contemporaries have sacrificed their hearts, minds, spirits, and bodies for, often against staggering odds. We must look beyond symbolic reverence and reclaim the essence of the Declaration that once defined the promise of our nation: "We hold these truths to be self-evident, that all men are created equal, that they are endowed by their Creator with certain unalienable Rights, that among these are Life, Liberty and the pursuit of Happiness."

The results of the 2024 US presidential election have made one thing undeniable: America stands at a defining moment. This nation and the global community must move beyond a survivalist mindset—one driven by self-interest, indulgence, and power—toward a vision of purposeful living. The question is no longer whether this nation can endure but whether it can uphold its existence by embracing a higher moral standard. History warns that civilizations unwilling to establish and uphold a moral blueprint for their populace to embrace ultimately collapse. If America continues down its path of division, complacency, and moral ambiguity, it will be no exception to this pattern of collapse.

The 2024 US presidential election revealed the deep fractures within the American society. Unity—already fragile—now seems even further out of reach. Political allegiance, economic status, race, gender, religion, and ideology continue to be the primary measures of credibility, relevance, and value. Power, authority, and prominence linked to this credibility, relevance, and value are still wielded for personal gain rather than for collective progress. Yet no nation can thrive without a shared moral foundation that its diverse populace can embrace. Without deliberate efforts to cultivate integrity, responsibility, and community through education, civic engagement, and cultural transformation, the growing divide will only deepen. The focus here is an assessment of a broken political system reflective of a fractured society.

The Pew Research Center has documented a sharp rise in partisan conflict since 1994, with the 2024 election underscoring these ideological rifts.

While political polarization is not new, today's divide has escalated into an existential clash over American identity and government responsibility. This fracture is most evident in three pivotal voter issues: the economy, women's health, and immigration. These divisions are not just shaping policy debates—they are redefining how Americans perceive their neighbors, institutions, and the very legitimacy of the democratic process.[101]

When political differences become the defining measure of American identity, self-interest, indulgence, and power take precedence over genuine governance. When relationships are shaped by these forces, power, authority, and prominence become ends in themselves, sought solely for credibility, relevance, and value. What remains absent is a shared moral foundation. Without a commitment to cultivating character through education, civic engagement, and cultural transformation, the divide between the legislative, executive, and judicial branches of government, as well as among the American people, will only grow wider.

Downgrading the American identity to political victories restricts achieving the American Dream to the powerful, the authoritarian, and the prominent. When considered without restrictions, the American identity would be expanded to encompass differences, various historical experiences, cultural influences, and democratic ideals. This unrestricted identity would embody freedom, equality, justice, and the rule of law for all Americans to experience. It would thrive on a diversity of cultures, races, ethnicities, and traditions. From the beginning of this nation's inception, the American identity would have encapsulated all Americans grounded in hard work, individualism, and determination to

---

[101] Yndira Marín, "Political Polarization in the 2024 US Presidential Election," LLYC, November 14, 2024, https://llyc.global/en/ideas/political-polarization-in-the-2024-u-s-presidential-election/.

achieve their dreams. The belief that any American can achieve success and prosperity regardless of their background emphasizes opportunity, freedom, and equality would have had genuine meaning. The American identity attached to being a leader in technological, social, and political advances would be a prideful achievement enjoyed by Americans in general. And rounding the corners of the American identity would have been its history and symbols, such as the American Revolution, the Civil Rights Movement, the Constitution, and the American flag. Once again, at the core of the American identity would be a collective belief in freedom, opportunity, and civic responsibility.

Without this collective belief firmly implanted in the hearts and minds of Americans, reforms essential to justice and progress, such as universal healthcare, fair labor standards, civil rights protections, gender equality, educational access, and environmental protections, are rendered inconsequential to the American identity. The rejection of these ideals is predictable in a society where character, integrity, and communal responsibility are not actively cultivated. During the 1530s, the renowned French writer Francois Rabelais stated in his series of books titled *Gargantua Pantagruel* the following: "Natura abhorret vacuum" (Nature abhors a vacuum). This generally accepted truism advances to the ensuing statement. When there exists a lack of development pertaining to a moral blueprint to fill a vacuum, the consequence is predictable. The guardrails that provide protection against the survivalist mindset motivated by self-interest, indulgence, and importance will be nonexistent.

The vacuum is filled with an obsession to secure power, authority, and prominence at any cost. Be it a relationship, family, culture, community, or nation, fracture and polarization ensues. If the 2024 US presidential election revealed anything, it exposed an American way of life that, from the beginning of its inception, began on a path that would ultimately amplify, to a large degree, a fractured and polarized society. This polarization has tangible effects on American society. Studies have found a correlation between heightened political discourse and increased political violence, suggesting that as partisan divisions intensify, so too does the potential for societal unrest.[102] America is at a breaking point. Without a renewed commitment to moral clarity, shared purpose, and the fundamental principles that define a just society, the divisions will not just persist—they will consume the very fabric of this nation.

The 2024 US presidential election also revealed just how broken the American political system is, and one classic strength for any democracy is voter participation. When registered voter apathy and disengagement occur during consequential elections, the democracy is weakened by allowing self-interest and importance to gain power, authority, and prominence over a system of living. There is an erosion of freedom, equality, justice, the rule of law, and diversity of cultures, races, ethnicities, and traditions. The Environmental Voter Project reported: "The 2024 election was in many ways a blow-out if you consider all the ballots that could have been cast but weren't. Using data from the University of Florida Election Lab, 85.9 million eligible voters skipped the 2024 general election. If "Did Not Vote" had been a presidential candidate, they would have beaten Donald Trump by 9.1 million votes, and they would have won twenty-one states, earning 265 Electoral College votes to Trump's 175 and Harris's 98."[103]

Though *The Guardian* reported more alarming numbers of apathetic and disengaged registered voters, the end result was the same. With a title beginning "What a Circus," the article shares that nearly 90 million Americans didn't vote—which is more than the number of

[102] Rachel Kleinfeld, "Polarization, Democracy, and Political Violence in the United States: What the Research Says," Carnegie Endowment for International Peace, September 5, 2023, https://carnegieendowment.org/research/2023/09/polarization-democracy-and-political-violence-in-the-united-states-what-the-research-says?lang=en.

[103] "2024 Was a Landslide . . . for 'Did Not Vote,'" Environmental Voter Project, November 25, 2024, https://www.environmentalvoter.org/updates/2024-was-landslidefor-did-not-vote.

people who voted for Trump or Harris.[104] For both the Environmental Project and *The Guardian*, reasons not to vote were consistent: vote did not matter due to the Electoral College system, politicians from both parties seemed unwilling to make the kind of fundamental economic and political changes that would make a meaningful difference for all people, no candidate represented working-class or middle-class interests of people, both parties were too similar and did not address concerns of the common voter, there seemed to be no point of voting, and aside from a handful of weaponized issues, the parties are nearly identical, and both parties hate the poor and serve only their donors.

The question deserves an answer: What has caused the American identity to lose its prestige and dissuaded millions of American registered voters from participating in the 2024 US presidential election? Understanding this failure is critical to preserving this nation's longevity, especially when elections are an important cornerstone of democracy. For the past years, the term MAGA—Make America Great Again—has dominated the media and thus the national landscape. In the minds of some Americans, one can only assume the time in the history of this nation when moments of greatness occurred was at the beginning of its inception. The Founding Fathers and landowning colleagues, who were all white males, held absolute power, authority, and prominence that shaped political, economic, military, and social systems to maintain their dominance.

During the ensuing years, other white males who were not necessarily landowners were allowed to join in the privilege and entitlement of possessing absolute power, authority, and prominence. Policies were enacted involving land ownership, slavery, and control of banking institutions to secure their all-encompassing dominance. Congress and the judiciary remained exclusively in their hands, ensuring that governance

---

[104] Jedidajah Otte, "What a Circus: Eligible US Voters on Why They Didn't Vote in the 2024 Presidential Election," *The Guardian*, December 13, 2024, https://www.theguardian.com/us-news/2024/dec/13/why-eligible-voters-did-not-vote.

served their interests. More policies were enacted, such as the westward expansion that displaced the Indigenous peoples, which further consolidated their wealth. Military power was used to justify territorial expansion at the expense of Native Americans. Military leadership also ensured continued white dominance and cemented white male authority.

The legal system reinforced their supremacy by upholding property rights and denying rights to women, enslaved Africans, and Indigenous communities. Court rulings, such as *Dred Scott v. Sandford* (1857), regulated racial exclusion and upheld white male privilege. Beyond politics, law, and the military, the white-male-controlled education, media, and religious institutions, shaping public discourse to sustain their dominance. Higher education remained exclusive, while newspapers and literature reflected elite values. Religious leaders often reinforced racial and gender hierarchies, justifying social inequalities through doctrine. At the expense of creating social, economic, military, and political imbalances that resulted from their moments to make America great, this did not hinder this faction of the populace from cherishing their absolute power, authority, and prominence.

Reflecting back during this early beginning, had the Founding Fathers and their landowning colleagues embraced their individual moral blueprints, a national moral blueprint would have naturally been established as the bedrock for this nation. It is unimaginable yet believable that a shared moral foundation for all living persons within this nation's borders would have been the precondition to circumvent the extreme polarization and disintegration this nation presently experiences. Once again, without a commitment to cultivate the characteristics that exemplify substantive character through education, civic engagement, and cultural transformation, the divide between the legislative, executive, and judicial branches of government, as well as among the American people, will only grow wider.

On the Tuesday evening of November 4, 2024, President Donald Trump gave the American people his State of the Union speech. The latter portion of his speech provided a window to observe his overall agenda. Of course, it was President Trump who years ago first coined the term "Make America Great Again" and ignited a faction of constituents who would like to reverse the spirit of Arabian folklore. For this faction of constituents, the American identity—which encompasses differences including varied historical experiences, cultural influences, and democratic ideals; embodies freedom, equality, justice, and the rule of law; and thrives on a diversity of cultures, races, ethnicities, and traditions—had gone too far. It was time to put the genie back into the bottle.

President Trump's closing remarks framed American greatness through the achievements of pioneers, warriors, and industrialists, crediting them with shaping the nation's strength and prosperity. He invokes imagery of ancestors crossing a vast ocean, venturing into the wilderness, and carving their fortunes from the land—language that elevates European settlers while erasing the brutal realities that made such expansion possible. This portrayal ignores the forced displacement and suffering of Native Americans, the foundational role of slavery in building the economy, and the sacrifices of women who fought for recognition and equality.

By glorifying conquest and struggle as an exclusively white, male-driven effort, his rhetoric dismisses the diverse and complex history of America. It suggests that true greatness belongs only to those who fit within this narrow vision, negating the contributions of those left out of his retelling. He calls on Americans to reclaim this legacy, vowing to usher in a new era of dominance, power, and expansion—one that mirrors the past he idealizes. By doing so, he reinforces a nostalgic longing for a time when control and prominence rested solely in the hands of white males like him, as well as women, who in the beginning benefited from this imbalance. Today, President Donald Trump declares that the "golden age of America has only just begun."

To grasp the political disintegration that has a perverse grasp upon this nation, it is important to first understand that it is merely a symptom of a greater problem and nothing more. A broken political system does not exist in isolation; it is often a reflection of deeper systemic failures across society. When politics become dysfunctional—serving the interests of the few rather than the many—other critical systems tend to mirror this collapse and reinforce cycles of inequality, corruption, and neglect.

Day after day, twenty-four hours a day through print, broadcast, digital, and online media such as newspapers, magazines, television and radio, and the internet, systemic failures across this nation are broadcast to a polarized and fragmented society. Ideally, while media is supposed to be unbiased, in reality, bias often exists. Different media outlets may present information in ways that reflect their perspectives, whether political, cultural, or corporate. Factors like ownership, audience demographics, and editorial policies influence how stories are framed. Ownership will reflect one of two perspectives, the survival mindset or the more progressive mindset.

The assumption can also be made that, in many ways, both biases perpetuate societal polarization and fragmentation. In a dysfunctional political system, propaganda replaces truth, and independent journalism is stifled. Without a well-informed citizenry, democratic participation declines, paving the way for authoritarian tendencies and unchecked corruption. Fortunately, there is a third perspective that represents a few media outlets that are known for in-depth, balanced reporting and strong investigative journalism that is considered unbiased. The *Christian Science Monitor, The Boston Globe, Reuters, Associated Press, BBC News, NPR* (National Public Radio), *The Wall Street Journal* (WSJ), *The Economist,* and *PBS NewsHour* would be examples.

Actively following the day-to-day reporting by the media outlets considered respectable and unbiased significantly helps an individual grasp an understanding of this nation's systemic failures. For example, socioeconomic failures do not exist in isolation; rather, they serve as major influences of political collapse. The economic system, which is often a reflection of political dysfunction, prioritizes corporate profits over workers' rights, deepening wealth inequality and limiting upward mobility. Policies that favor deregulation and tax cuts for the wealthy create an economic structure that benefits a select few while leaving the majority struggling with stagnant wages and rising living costs. The financial obsession with the bottom line of industries, where profits take precedence over labor, further erodes economic stability, as wealth concentrates at the top and leaves the working and middle classes increasingly vulnerable.

Adding to this disparity is the nation's judicial system, which parallels political failures when laws are applied unequally, favoring the powerful while excessively punishing the marginalized communities. For example, mass incarcerations, racial profiling, and sentencing disparities demonstrate how legal frameworks are manipulated to maintain social hierarchies rather than to uphold justice. Political leaders who fail to address systemic injustices in law enforcement and the courts effectively sanction a two-tiered justice system, where privilege dictates outcomes rather than fairness.

Consistently broadcasted is this nation's failing educational system. No matter what political party is in power, this is just another symptom of the government's unwillingness to invest in a curriculum that virtuously creates an informed and empowered masses. Underfunded schools, disparities in access to quality education, and the ever-rising cost of higher education perpetuate the belief that knowledge remains a privilege rather than a right. This lack of investment in education perpetuates generational cycles of poverty and ignorance while maintaining power, authority, and prominent configurations that benefit from an uninformed electorate. When governments fail to prioritize equitable education, they deliberately create masses that are less equipped to challenge the powerful, authoritative, and prominent to demand systemic change.

Much has been discussed regarding this nation's healthcare systems, which also bear the scars of political neglect. Privatization, exorbitant costs, and disparities in medical treatment continue to expose a government more invested in profit than in public well-being. Time after time, the voices of appeal keep disclosing when access to healthcare becomes a privilege rather than a fundamental right, the social fabric weakens. As a result, preventable illnesses and financial ruin become common experiences. A society that cannot provide for the basic health needs of its citizens fosters widespread cynicism and distrust in political leadership, which further erodes stability.

With the current decline regarding the importance of diversity in the workplace, the social and racial climate has been adversely impacted. Decades of progression within the social and racial sectors are reduced to reforms judged as inconsequential. Justice systems will once again be exposed to practices of gender inequality, discrimination, and voter suppression. These practices are often used to maintain existing power, authority, and prominent structures rather than to dismantle them. When relegated communities are systematically disenfranchised, the democratic process is rendered hollow, and the legitimacy of governance is called into question.

The list of socioeconomic failures concludes with this nation's electoral system that continues to expose political dysfunction when gerrymandering, voter suppression, and unchecked corporate funding are allowed to undermine the democratic process. When elections are manipulated to favor entrenched power, citizens lose faith in their ability to effect change through democratic means. As earlier recorded from a sample of the 85.9 to 90 million eligible American voters who skipped the 2024 presidential election general election, this disillusionment breeds apathy or radicalization, further destabilizing governance. The voter descent bears repeating:

> My vote did not matter due to the Electoral College system; politicians from both parties seemed unwilling to make the kind of fundamental economic and political changes that would make a meaningful difference for all people; no candidate represented working- or middle-class interests of people; both parties were too similar and did not address concerns of the common voter; there is no point in voting; aside from a handful of weaponized issues, the parties are nearly identical, and both parties hate the poor and serve only their donors.

What has become quite evident is that this nation's broken political system is, therefore, both a cause and result of this nation's other institutional failures. Overall, when leadership prioritizes power, authority, and prominence over people, these same institutions meant to serve society become nothing more than instruments of control rather than focused on authentically based progress. Readily observed are indiscriminate mass layoffs and terminations taking place to save the bottom line of institutions, and many of this nation's institutions have grown indifferent to the suffering of their fellow citizens. This is not the destiny Americans of all races, colors, traditions, and backgrounds were expecting when adapting to the American identity.

True reforms that elevate the entire society require addressing these interconnected crises, which means fixing the political system alone is not enough. Economic, judicial, educational, and social institutions require a restructuring with equity, justice, and accountability at their core. Without systemic change, political collapse is not just a possibility—it is an inevitability.

Today, America stands before its "day of reckoning" due to a decision to establish power, authority, and prominence as primary means to achieve credibility, relevance, and value. As a consequence of this decision, moral decay and national uncertainty hold this nation in its vicelike grips. America currently stands at a decisive crossroads. The choice before this nation is unequivocally clear: Remain complacent and watch this beloved nation crumble or rise to the occasion with a renewed sense of commitment to live a higher moral standard. History has revealed the collapse of prior civilizations due to the refusal to establish a moral blueprint equivalent to the importance of power, authority, and prominence. However, history has also revealed that civilizations thrive and experience unremitting longevity when guided by principles of integrity, justice, and collective responsibility.

This is America's defining moment. The path forward requires courage, discipline, and an unwavering belief in the importance of developing a higher moral standard that recognizes the inherent value of all Americans regardless of race, color, traditions and background. What is the decisive move for our nation to take at this defining moment? A rejection of the practices that base power, authority, and prominence as the sole means to define credibility, relevance, and value is imperative if restoration of our nation's American identity is to experience a rebirth. In truth, the fate of our society hinges on the moral choices made today.

This nation was built on ideals—freedom, justice, and the pursuit of a better future that originally was targeted for a select few. That is not the case today. These ideals cannot be intended to involve a select few if this nation is to avoid a depraved collapse. Without a strong, principled foundation reflective of a moral blueprint, these ideals risk becoming hollow. To this date, in the history of America, corruption, greed, and self-interest have infiltrated the highest levels of our institutions, and as stated, many have grown indifferent to the suffering of their fellow citizens. This is not the destiny Americans were meant to accept. Together, Americans are challenged to fight for something greater. Together, Americans are challenged to claim the moral principles that were initially proclaimed by a few but now are claimed by all of its inhabitants for the purpose of making this nation great for the correct motives.

How does this nation arrive at a principled foundation reflective of a moral blueprint? Begin with elevating the educational system to teach an individual to recognize, develop, and practice the inherent qualities they entered this life possessing. Educating a person to value such qualities that exemplify their substantive character accomplishes one certain result. That same individual learns firsthand that a higher moral standard is not just an abstract concept. They learn that such qualities of sound character are the guiding force that can lead an individual, and certainly a country, out of periods culminating in darkness.

At hand, there is a solution that supports the will-to-live ideology. However, this sort of learning effort requires sacrifice, accountability, and a willingness to challenge the status quo, which is in opposition to a survivalist mindset. This mindset will consistently support the exertion of power, authority, and prominence to resolve dissimilarities. Americans have the right to expect integrity from their leaders, justice in the laws of the land, and fairness in our economy. Most importantly, Americans have a right to hold one another accountable to the same principles expected from leadership. True change will always begin with personal responsibility.

Throughout the history of this nation, there have been great movements fueled by individuals refusing to cast aside their moral standards, even at the cost of their lives. For example, Nathan Hale (1755–1776), Medgar Evers (1925–1963), Dr. Martin Luther King Jr. (1929–1968), Joan Trumpauer Mulholland (b. 1941), Harriet Tubman (c. 1822–1913), Ida B. Wells (1862–1931), Viola Liuzzo (1925–1965), and Mary Dyer (1611–1660). Included amongst this list are the abolitionists who fought against slavery to the civil rights leaders who stood against injustice. It is remarkable how moral progress in this nation has persistently depended on individuals who upheld the highest ethical standards, even in the face of adversity. The time has arrived that more Americans follow in their footsteps, rather than the footsteps of the original founding few who chose to be silent in the presence of corruption and moral decay.

To personally embrace the will-to-live ideology instead of a survival mindset will be difficult and intense. Once power, authority, and prominence have become a coveted personal conviction to experience, it is difficult to relinquish their seductive self-interest and indulgence. However, the potential to absorb oneself inside the effervesce of self-importance, so, too, is the greater potential to bask in the collective importance of this nation.

To commit to developing a societal curriculum that educates an individual to recognize, develop, and practice the very best inherent qualities each person brings into this life, helps this society to embrace a higher moral standard and will thus reshape this nation for the better. With this new style of learning, Americans can rebuild trust in our institutions, strengthen our communities, and create a future where honesty, fairness, and compassion are the cornerstones of our national identity. This is not an impossible dream; it is a necessary course of action.

Unity, rather than polarization, calls for the type of action that elevates this populace to rise above cynicism and moral apathy, which weakened our nation. The time has also arrived to take personal responsibility to inspire future generations to believe in something greater than self-interest, indulgence, and importance. The road ahead will not be easy, but at this stage in American history, it is the only path worth taking. The fate of this nation depends on the moral choices its populace makes today and tomorrow.

Chapter 8

A CIVIC'S RENEWAL

———————✿———————

Democracy itself is a moral enterprise, one that depends on the active participation of morally responsible citizens. American factional hostility is only a detriment to society.

—Jean Bethke Elshtain

Individuals and societies are prone to self-deception and the pursuit of their own advantage, often justifying it as moral or necessary.

—Anonymous

As our nation stands on the precipice of change, the necessity of accepting moral responsibility for ourselves and toward one another has never been clearer. In the previous chapters, the path forward has been outlined. It is a path grounded in the restoration of ethical values and the collective will to rebuild what has been lost, the dignity of humankind. Now, as the final stage of this journey has been reached, it is essential to recognize that the time for reflection has passed. The question is no longer whether this nation will act, but how. How do Americans instill the moral clarity necessary to rescue our nation from the brink of collapse? How do we, as individuals and as a society, claim the virtues of substantive character that have long been overlooked as a vital means that sustains this nation's longevity?

The need for moral renewal is not a new idea for an individual or society. Throughout history, renowned philosophers and leaders have endorsed the call for an ethical society. The ancient Greek philosopher Aristotle, for instance, argued that the key to a well-functioning society was the cultivation of virtue—a habit, developed over time, that shapes the character of individuals and the broader community. Aristotle believed that a virtuous life was essential for human flourishing and that moral character was not a matter of chance but of choice. His philosophy teaches us that virtue is something we must actively cultivate, not just in times of crisis, but as a daily practice.[105]

In a similar vein, the American philosopher, psychologist, and educational reformer John Dewey emphasized the importance of moral education in fostering a democratic society. Dewey argued that education should not just focus on academic subjects but on developing the moral character needed for civic engagement. His belief that "democracy needs to be built upon a moral foundation" speaks directly to the challenges we face today in rebuilding a society that values ethical principles.[106]

In the twentieth century, Dr. Martin Luther King Jr. provided an excellent example that championed the idea of moral clarity in the face of injustice. Dr. King's call for nonviolent resistance was not just a political strategy; it was a moral imperative. He contended that the time to act morally was always "right," reminding us that doing what is right is not contingent on convenience or timing but on the unwavering

[105] Anselm H. Amadio and Anthony J.P. Kenny, "The Lyceum of Aristotle," Britannica, Last updated April 14, 2025, https://www.britannica.com/biography/Aristotle/The-Lyceum.

[106] Elizabeth Anderson, "Dewey's Moral Philosophy," *The Stanford Encyclopedia of Philosophy*, Edward N. Zalta & Uri Nodelman (eds.), https://plato.stanford.edu/entries/dewey-moral/.

commitment to justice. His teachings remind us that moral leadership is not about avoiding conflict but about confronting evil with courage and compassion. Dr. King's ability to unite people from diverse backgrounds around the idea of moral integrity shows that ethical movements can transcend differences and unite us around shared values.[107]

No longer can the importance of moral integrity be buried in theoretical language or based on past abstractions to be effective. The renewal has to be a living, breathing necessity for the survival of our society. Overcoming the damaging effects of self-interest and indulgence is essential to uniting a diverse society and safeguarding democracy. Coauthors Debra Erickson and Michael Le Chevallier compiled a collection of essays that meticulously examined the work of one of America's leading political theorists and public intellectuals, the celebrated Jean Bethke Elshtain. In their book *Jean Bethke Elshtain: Politics, Ethics, and Society,* authors Erickson and Le Chevallier maintained a focus on her key themes of politics, ethics, religion, international relations, and the ends of political life.[108]

One distinguished contributor for the compilations was Nancy J. Hirschmann, a Geraldine R. Segal Professor in American Social Thought at the School of Arts & Sciences, University of Pennsylvania. In Professor Hirschmann's contributing essay in Chapter 5 of the book, she examines Jean Bethke Elshtain's perspective on democracy, highlighting her belief that it must exist between extreme individualism and collectivism. Elshtain rejects the idea that democracy is simply a numbers game, where the majority's preferences dictate outcomes without any real engagement in the common good. She argues that democracy

---

[107] John Brown, "The Time Is Always Right to Do What Is Right: How MLK's Famous Quote Applies to the Barbershop Experience," Joe Black Barbershop, https://www.joeblackbarbershop.com/the-time-is-always-right-to-do-what-is-right-how-mlks-famous-quote-applies-to-the-barbershop-experience/.

[108] Debra Erickson and Michael Le Chevallier, *Jean Bethke Elshtain: Politics, Ethics, and Society* (Notre Dame, IN: University of Notre Dame Press, 2018).

requires conversation, respect for differences, and a shared commitment to policies that benefit society as a whole.

Yet, when Elshtain wrote *Democracy on Trial*, she expressed deep anxiety about the state of democracy, worried that it was deteriorating under the weight of political cynicism and disengagement. Hirschmann, rereading Elshtain's work years later, found that her concerns have only become more relevant, and she admitted to feeling just as nervous about democracy's decline. The erosion of trust in institutions, the rise of self-serving political leadership, and the sense that ordinary citizens no longer have a voice have only reinforced the dangers Elshtain warned about years ago.[109]

Hirschmann expands on Elshtain's concerns by reflecting on how democracy has continued to unravel. She describes a growing frustration among citizens who feel that their votes no longer matter, as politicians cater more to wealthy donors than to the people they represent. Elshtain believed that democracy should empower individuals to actively participate in shaping their society, yet Hirschmann sees a system where people feel increasingly powerless. She notes that for Elshtain, democracy was always more than just a political system—it was a moral project, requiring citizens to take responsibility for one another and resist the forces that divide and isolate them.

She does not deny the importance of difference, especially within a civic body. The future of our democracy rests not just on voting or political engagement but on a deep, abiding commitment to ethical action in all facets of life. However, in today's climate of polarization and distrust, Hirschmann worries that the moral fabric necessary for a thriving democracy is fraying. Like Elshtain, she longs for a renewal of

---

[109] Nancy Hirschmann, "Democracy, Depression, and Disability: Jean Elshtain on Democracy, Despair, and Hope," in *Jean Bethke Elshtain: Politics, Ethics, and Society*, Debra Erickson and Michael Le Chevallier eds. (IN: University of Notre Dame Press, 2018).

civic engagement and a deeper commitment to the common good, but she struggles to see where that revival might begin.

Finally, Hirschmann offers disability rights activism as a model for revitalizing democracy. Unlike other identity movements, she argues, disability activism has successfully fostered bipartisan policy changes, such as the Americans with Disabilities Act, by emphasizing inclusivity and collective problem-solving. While Elshtain was skeptical of identity politics, Hirschmann sees the disability movement as an example of how democracy can work when citizens mobilize effectively. Despite her concerns about the state of democracy, Hirschmann concludes that hope lies in small, incremental actions that promote inclusion, civic responsibility, and meaningful engagement.[110]

In her own book, *Democracy on Trial*, Jean Bethke Elshtain argues: "We confront one another as aggrieved groups rather than as free citizens. Cynicism, boredom, apathy, despair, and violence have become a coin of the civic realm. They are dark signs of the times and a warning that democracy may not be up to the task of satisfying the yearnings it unleashes—yearnings for freedom, fairness, and equality. A functioning democracy requires not only participation but moral courage, a willingness to challenge injustice and advocate for the common good, even when it is difficult."[111]

But perhaps the most urgent lesson we can draw comes from history itself. When faced with moral crises, societies have turned to leaders who exemplified moral courage and integrity. One of the most compelling examples is the abolitionist movement in the United States. Figures like Frederick Douglass and Harriet Tubman, who fought against the moral atrocity of slavery, demonstrate how a moral revival can be sparked by the courage of a few. Douglass's 1852 "What to the Slave Is the Fourth

---

[110] Hirschmann, "Democracy, Depression, and Disability," 104–114.

[111] Jean Bethke Elshtain, *Democracy on Trial* (Toronto, ON: House of Anansi Press, 2003).

of July?" speech delivered in the Corinthian Hall, Rochester, New York, demonstrated unbridled courage when he stated:

> Oppression makes a wise man mad. With brave men there is always a remedy for oppression. I have said that the Declaration of Independence is the ringbolt to the chain of your nation's destiny; so, indeed, I regard it. The principles contained in that instrument are saving principles. Stand by those principles, be true to them on all occasions, in all places, against all foes, and at whatever cost. Are the great principles of political freedom and of natural justice embodied in that Declaration of Independence extended to us?
>
> But, such is not the state of the case. I say it with a sad sense of the disparity between us. I am not included within the pale of this glorious anniversary! Your high independence only reveals the immeasurable distance between us. This Fourth of July is yours, not mine. You may rejoice, 1 must mourn. To drag a man in fetters into the grand illuminated temple of liberty, and call upon him to join you in joyous anthems, were inhuman mockery and sacrilegious irony.
>
> Do you mean, citizens, to mock me by asking me to speak today? If so, there is a parallel to your Conduct. And let me warn you that it is dangerous to copy the example of a nation whose crimes, towering up to heaven, were thrown down by the breath of the Almighty, burying that nation in irrecoverable ruin! I can today take up the plaintive lament of a peeled and woe-smitten people! Fellow citizens, above your national, tumultuous joy, I hear the mournful wail of millions, whose chains, heavy

and grievous yesterday, are, today, rendered more intolerable by the jubilee shouts that reach them.

If I do forget, if I do not faithfully remember those bleeding children of sorrow this day, " may my right hand forget her cunning, and may my tongue cleave to the roof of my mouth !" To forget them, to pass lightly over their wrongs, and to chime in with the popular theme, would be treason most scandalous and shocking and would make me a reproach before God and the world. My subject, then, fellow citizens, is American Slavery. I shall see this day, and its popular characteristics, from the slave's point of view. Standing, there, identified with the American bondman, making his wrongs mine, I do not hesitate to declare, with all my soul, that the character and conduct of this nation never looked blacker to me than on this 4th of July![112]

Throughout Frederick Douglass's autobiography, he reveals the merit of moral transformation when he recognized the injustice of slavery and began to commit himself to the abolition movement. His powerful narrative reminds us that the fight for moral justice requires unwavering commitment, but that it is, above all, a fight for human dignity.[113]

At this point, when this writer had concluded reading Frederick Douglass's Fourth of July speech and autobiography, I was soberly reminded of Professor Hirschmann and Jean Elshtain's concerns, feeling nervous regarding our democracy. Today, we face a similar challenge

---

[112] Frederick Douglass, "What to the Slave Is the Fourth of July?" Internet Archive, full speech transcript, https://archive.org/stream/Douglass_July_Oration/ocm30553533_V_0_djvu.txt.

[113] Frederick Douglass, *Life and Times of Frederick Douglass: His Early Life as a Slave, His Escape from Bondage, and His Complete History* (New York: Collier Books, 1962).

Frederick Douglass describes as missing during his era: Our nation is in need of a moral awakening. The breakdown of ethical values has led to widespread cynicism, as well as stark and hostile polarization. Yet, as our great thinkers and movements that have elevated our nation have shown, moral revivals are possible. The Women's Suffrage Movement (19th–20th century), Labor Movement (19th–20th century), Civil Rights Movement (1950s–1960s), and Abolitionist Movement (18th–19th century) pushed our nation closer to its ideals of liberty, justice, and equality. Now is not the time to allow self-interest and indulgence to continue dominating our humanity to increasing degrees that further push our society to the point of self-destruction.

Though sporadically, what we have learned from our own history is that when individuals act with integrity, when communities demand justice, and when we look to the teachings of those who came before us for guidance, the moral landscape dramatically shifts upwards. It is amazing how little humanity has learned from history regarding the predominant reason for the collapse of previous civilizations. This inability to grasp how the lack or degeneration of a moral foundation is the leading cause for the collapse of previous civilizations speaks volumes as to how power, authority, and prominence, once absorbed, are extremely intoxicating. For a more thorough examination of how and when this particular phenomenon initially took place, examine the book written by this writer titled: *Trust the Confession: Disavow Ignorance for Personal Freedom.*

A nation, society, community, family, or relationship lacking a moral blueprint is predictably vulnerable to disorder, corruption, and decay. Why? Because, in the absence of moral guidance, the pursuit of power and prominence overshadows the inherent qualities of character that every individual possesses at birth. A moral blueprint is representative of these qualities. This blueprint becomes a foundation to ensure that qualities such as integrity, responsibility, and respect are demonstrated toward every person, regardless of socio-economic differences.

Reaffirming civic education in the home, schools, workplaces, places of worship, and community meetings plays a significant role in reinforcing this moral foundation. By teaching a populace their rights, responsibilities, and the importance of ethical governance, civic education can help inspire a sense of duty toward one another; again, regardless of socioeconomic differences. Without this education, individuals may drift toward apathy or, worse, abuse power in pursuit of self-interest and self-indulgence, leading to the breakdown of societal institutions.

When a person recognizes, develops, and practices their inherent moral qualities, they cultivate attributes that lead to community, leadership, humility, and compassion. These same qualities not only strengthen personal character but also foster a society rooted in cooperation, service, and ethical leadership. Rather than pursuing self-interest and indulgence at the expense of others, an individual can grow into roles of responsibility with a sense of duty and fairness, ensuring that influence is exercised for the benefit of all.

Reintroducing civic education across all aspects of society, homes, schools, workplaces, places of worship, and community gatherings is fundamental to reinforcing a moral blueprint throughout our society. This act ensures that future generations will develop a sense of duty, justice, and service, preventing moral decay and potential collapse. Instead, this act can promote within our nation a standard of leadership defined by wisdom, integrity, and a commitment to the common fact that "all men and women are created equal, that they are endowed by their Creator with certain unalienable Rights, that among these are Life, Liberty and the pursuit of Happiness."

One positive outcome that has not been discussed regarding civic education is the opportunity for an individual to define themselves by a different metric, one rooted in inherent moral qualities rather than solely by experiences. Training individuals to recognize, develop, and practice these qualities of substance allows them to separate from both negative and positive experiences. Maintaining a sense of duty toward oneself and others—rooted in cooperation, service, and ethical leadership while facing personal triumphs or setbacks—is a decisive rejection of harmful patterns passed down through generations. When individuals lack education and training regarding the substantive attributes that exemplify the best within them, separation from past experiences, whether negative or positive, becomes impossible.

Exposure to civic education validates Aristotle's assertion: "We become just by doing just acts, temperate by doing temperate acts, brave by doing brave acts."[114] He affirms that substantive character is cultivated that exemplifies inherent qualities. The benefit of civic training is that it teaches an individual that virtue is developed through habitual actions. Thus, the moral strength of our nation is truly a reflection of the choices Americans make each day. It is through a commitment to moral education and the conscious practice of virtue that individuals, and by extension, society, develop an ethical foundation necessary for a fair and enduring nation.

America remains a challenged nation to revamp its system of measurement that links power, authority, and prominence to credibility, relevance, and value. Because of this dominant system, America is often consumed with persistent disparities involving economic class, gender, race, education, access to healthcare, age, disability, and criminal justice. For example, there is a prevailing belief that America is a racist nation. However, what is commonly overlooked is an understanding that socioeconomic disparities produced by practices of discrimination, bias, prejudice, bigotry, injustice, or unfairness indicate symptoms that represent a prominent societal malaise.

Lacking a system of measurement characteristic of a moral blueprint, institutions based on power, authority, and prominence remain the primary explanations for socioeconomic disparities. Prioritizing integrity, service, and the well-being of others through a curriculum

---

[114] Aristotle, *Nicomachean Ethics Books II-IV*, trans. C.C.W. Taylor (Oxford: Oxford University Press, 2006), 2.

focused on civic education would establish credibility and relevance more authentically. This counterbalance would also create opportunities for individuals committed to unpretentious leadership to emerge. A well-structured moral blueprint would measure trustworthiness, accountability, empathy, compassion, generosity, influence, and ethical courage as legitimate indicators of credibility, relevance, and value. This shift would ensure that influence is based not on dominance, but on substantive character, service, and societal impact, creating a moral foundation for our nation's renewal.

Once again, our nation faces a crucial challenge: Will we embrace moral responsibility as a fundamental practice, or will we continue ignoring it in favor of self-interest, indulgence, and status? Either moral responsibility takes root in our institutions, or America risks following the fate of past civilizations—ultimate collapse. Recognizing the need for change is no longer enough; we must actively engage in rebuilding a moral foundation that can sustain the longevity of our nation. Every American must ask themselves: Are we, individually and collectively, willing to sacrifice for the moral sustainability of this country, or will we continue prioritizing convenience, selfishness, and moral indifference?

As stated in Chapter 6, I once asked myself as a young man, "What the hell is character?" No one had ever talked to me about character. During my developmental years, I was told to behave, respect my elders, and demonstrate good manners. The consequences for failing to do so were either confinement to the house or corporal punishment. So I learned to adjust, behaving in ways that pleased those who held power, authority, and prominence over me. However, rather than being guided to recognize and develop the qualities of good character that I inherently possessed, I instead adapted to a societal practice of portraying myself as a good person while simultaneously internalizing the power dynamics modeled by those around me. Relationships became defined by a struggle for power, rather than by a sense of moral duty or integrity. Without a moral blueprint, something civic education could have provided, renewal was impossible.

Civic education helps an individual to recognize and appreciate their best qualities while also valuing similar qualities of strength in others. When such an education is absent in our society's agenda, the outcry of "What the hell is character?" becomes all too understandable. It is common knowledge that family is the foundational unit of society, and that within the home, a child should learn honor, responsibility, and respect for others. However, when civic education is lacking, and the prevailing societal message emphasizes the pursuit of power, authority, and prominence above all else, the outcome is predictable: a weakening of society. The absence of a counterbalance between the will to survive and the will to live with purpose and integrity becomes an impediment to moral progress. In our culture, where superficial standards of success often outweigh ethical behavior, it is critical to teach a child not just to achieve, but to achieve with integrity.

John Dewey, the American philosopher, psychologist, and educational reformer, was one of the most influential scholars of the early twentieth century. He was a strong advocate for extending moral education beyond academics, urging families and communities to create environments where the values of citizenship and empathy could thrive. In his book *Moral Principles in Education*, Dewey emphasizes the school's responsibility to develop students' moral character:

> The business of the educator, whether parent or teacher, is to see to it that the greatest possible number of ideas acquired by children and youth are acquired in such a vital way that they become moving ideas, motive-forces in the guidance of conduct. This demand and this opportunity make the moral purpose universal and dominant in all instruction, whatever the topic. The moral responsibility of the school, and of those who conduct

it, is to society. The school is fundamentally an institution erected by society to do a certain specific work—to exercise a certain specific function in maintaining the life and advancing the welfare of society. The educational system which does not recognize that this fact entails upon it an ethical responsibility is derelict and a defaulter. It is not doing what it was called into existence to do.

Dewey further asserts:

The social work of the school is often limited to training for citizenship, and citizenship is then interpreted in a narrow sense as meaning the capacity to vote intelligently and the disposition to obey laws. But it is futile to contract and cramp the ethical responsibility of the school in this way. The child is an organic whole—intellectually, socially, and morally, as well as physically.

We must take the child as a member of society in the broadest sense and demand for and from the schools whatever is necessary to enable the child to intelligently recognize all his social relations and take his part in sustaining them. The child is to be not only a voter and a subject of law; he is also to be a member of a family and, in all probability, responsible for the rearing and training of future children, thereby maintaining the continuity of society.

The child ought to have the same motives for right doing and to be judged by the same standards in the school as the adult in the wider social life to which he belongs. Interest in community welfare, an interest that is intellectual and practical, as well as emotional an interest, that is to say, in perceiving whatever makes for social order and progress, and in carrying these principles into execution is the moral habit to which all the special school habits must be related if they are to be animated by the breath of life.[115]

Few would argue with Dewey's belief that parents and teachers must ensure that a child acquires ideas that become "moving ideas" guiding their conduct. In theory, he is correct. However, in practice, his vision is overly idealistic. This is where my perspective diverges from Dewey's.

Dewey asserts that "the moral responsibility of the school, and of those who conduct it, is to society." But what happens when society itself lacks a moral blueprint? Without a foundational moral directive, society becomes dominated by a "will-to-survive" ideology, in which power, authority, and prominence become the ultimate goals for people to achieve. As a result, the very society Dewey entrusts with moral education becomes the number-one architect for generating disparities, such as school funding inequities, limited access to advanced courses, inconsistent teacher quality and availability, and biases in standardized testing.

I do not disagree with Dewey's statement that "the school is fundamentally an institution erected by society to do a certain specific work, to exercise a certain specific function in maintaining the life and advancing the welfare of society." Theoretically, this is true. But without a moral blueprint to guide it, this goal remains unattainable. The lack of civic training in schools and the broader American culture means that, rather than counterbalancing intense polarization, education often reinforces it. Society, dominated by a will-to-survive mindset, serves as a model for schools to replicate division rather than unity. Without a moral foundation to aspire to, Dewey's claim that "the child ought

---

[115] John Dewey, *Moral Principles in Education* (New York: Houghton Mifflin Company, 1909).

to have the same motives for right-doing" remains nothing more than wishful thinking. How can children be expected to prioritize ethical behavior when the society shaping them is consumed with self-interest, indulgence, and the pursuit of status at the expense of others?

Moral courage, as demonstrative of its foundation, extends beyond family and school structures. Just as important is moral courage necessary in the community, such as in the workplace. To assure that power, authority, and prominence are counterbalanced with integrity, this courage must not only be a personal practice but a collective responsibility. Pulitzer Prize writer and leadership theorist James MacGregor Burns states: "Transformational leadership occurs when one or more persons engage with others in such a way that leaders and followers raise one another to higher levels of motivation and morality."[116]

When ethical behavior is modeled by individuals in power, this moral courage establishes a standard for everyone in the organization that creates a culture that values both achievement and moral integrity. When individuals in power lead by example, prioritizing honesty, fairness, and respect, an environment is created where these values penetrate through every level of operation. A business culture where ethics and profit go hand in hand is not only possible but necessary for lasting success and societal well-being.[117]

However, it is not enough to simply focus on personal morality or community action alone. The institutions that govern our society must also reflect shared ethical ideals. From SparkNotes:

> As philosopher Immanuel Kant argued in his *Critique of Practical Reason*, moral action is not just an individual responsibility; it extends to the collective structures that govern us. He proposes a method for teaching morality.

---

[116] James MacGregor Burns, *Leadership* (New York: Open Road Media, 2012).

[117] Theo Winter, "In A Nutshell: Transformational Leadership," Human Performance Technology, May 2, 2014, https://blog.hptbydts.com/in-a-nutshell-transformational-leadership.

It is essential to teach the student to act from duty and not merely outwardly conform to morality. Kant recommends that we enlist our pupil's natural delight in debating ethical matters and allow them to develop their judgment by evaluating various moral actions. He warns against presenting overblown heroism as a moral ideal, as it does not prepare students for everyday ethical challenges, or portraying morality merely as a practical tool, which would prevent them from appreciating morality for its own sake. By presenting examples of moral law acting independently, the student learns how moral law can free them from being enslaved by personal desires.[118]

Kant emphasizes that individuals must consider whether their actions could be applied universally to benefit all, particularly in political and socioeconomic contexts. Such considerations ensure that laws and institutions are designed with fairness, equity, and justice as their foundation. When political leaders and legislators uphold principles of justice, equality, and respect for human dignity, they cultivate an environment where society as a whole can flourish. Kant also recognized the importance of establishing a moral blueprint to act as a foundation that would include all constituents of society.

This distinction underscores the unique role of practical reason in guiding moral action, independent of pragmatic and utilitarian considerations. It challenges those who judge morality solely based on outcomes, arguing instead that an action's morality is determined by the principle on which it is performed. Teaching individuals to recognize, develop, and practice their best inherent qualities establishes a moral

---

[118] Immanuel Kant, Sparknote for *Critique of Practical Reason*, https://www.sparknotes.com/philosophy/practical reason/summary/.

blueprint based on principle, one in which all members of society can thrive, ensuring long-term sustainability.

The call for moral renewal that our nation is challenged to accept is not simply a theoretical or idealistic undertaking. To the contrary, it is a practical and essential appeal that pertains to the survival of our democracy. From the family to the community, to the workplace, and to other institutions, it is time we take concrete actions to implement moral clarity. John Dewey, James Burns, Immanuel Kant, and countless preceding distinguished thinkers have offered noble suggestions for establishing moral clarity, which is essential for the sustainability of an individual and of democracy.

This means actively teaching, modeling, and demanding ethical behavior in every sphere of life. Waiting for a perfect system or society to emerge is naïve and passive; we must build it, step-by-step, through our daily actions and interactions. If America is to awaken fully to adopt a moral blueprint that it has lacked since its founding, where all constituents of this nation can flourish, then we must focus on creating moral education that empowers individuals to make ethical choices benefiting both themselves and the broader community. Repetition is a necessary component of learning. Therefore, by instilling and reinforcing moral development, we create a foundation where all members of society can thrive.

Categorically, we cannot afford to be naïve about this moral revival journey. Without question, this renewal will be met with resistance. There are factions in our society that thrive on moral decay, division, and hostile fragmentation. Others profit from inequality, dishonesty, and a lack of accountability. These same forces will fight against any movement that threatens their power, authority, and prominence. Elevating our educational curriculum to include civic and moral training will undoubtedly be seen as a direct threat. Teaching individuals, whether children or adults, to recognize, develop, and embody the best qualities of character they inherently possess upon entering this life will face vehement opposition.

Supporters of the will-to-survive ideology will not easily allow it to be counterbalanced by the will-to-live ideology. Yet history has shown, time and again, that moral movements are often born out of struggle. The abolitionists, the suffragists, the civil rights activists, the labor movement, the Native American rights movement, and the disability rights movement all faced formidable opposition. But through unwavering commitment to justice and moral clarity, they brought about transformative change.

This time, such a transformation cannot afford to be minimized in terms of importance. The resolve for advocating for the will-to-live ideology is due to this way of life being grounded in moral law, not self-interest, indulgence, or the pursuit of power. As stated, supporters for this ideology will be vigorously challenged. However, the willingness to honorably confront resistance, challenge the status quo, and stand firm in the conviction that a just society is worth fighting for validates the will-to-live ideology. The mandate to educate, engage, and awaken individuals who have been taught that moral clarity is secondary to personal gain is a powerful directive. It is imperative to know—the moral foundation of our nation is not merely an abstract ideal but a fundamental necessity for the survival of our democracy.

Again, history has not been shy with its dictate. Time and time again, societies that abandon ethical principles eventually deteriorate due to "eating their own." In reference to societal collapse, "eating its own" translates to when the general population turns against itself. Corruption, dishonesty, and the erosion of communal trust weaken the foundations necessary for prosperity to be a collective experience. Examples would be political polarization, economic disparity, and institutional distrust that stem from a decline in a moral blueprint. These are signs that a society is consuming itself from within rather than addressing external or internal challenges in a practical manner. Regrettably, these same signs that forecast collapse are currently engulfing our populace throughout our American culture.

This chapter explores how a higher moral standard can be developed as a guiding blueprint to save our nation from collapse, emphasizing personal responsibility, collective ethics, and leadership integrity as the foundations of a stable society. It is common knowledge that no government or institution can legislate morality effectively; it must be embraced on an individual basis. Each American can be accountable for their actions, striving for honesty, fairness, and respect. Without this personal commitment, our nation's moral renewal is impossible. Civic and moral education that emphasizes the recognition and value regarding the best attributes of character an individual inherently possesses can be made available to an adult or child. Once embraced, this form of education can morally catapult our nation beyond the reach of the survival mindset obsessed with self-interest, indulgence, and importance.

Thus far, we have petitioned society as a whole—homes, schools, workplaces, places of worship, and community gatherings—to join in this campaign to initiate a moral revival into this nation's way of life. However, it is extremely important that we petition the media and entertainment industries to also join in our campaign. Why? It is quite obvious. The media and entertainment industries hold significant leverage in shaping public perception and societal values.

When factions of the American culture give precedence to materialism, sensationalism, and instant gratification over principles of integrity and perseverance, the outcome is predictable. This type of precedence, which represents a survivalist mindset, weakens the collective moral compass. The media and entertainment industries can do their part to counterbalance this misguided priority by highlighting positive role models, ethical dilemmas, and stories of moral courage that reinforce the importance of virtue in everyday life.

Finally, moral renewal requires a fundamental shift in how we define success as a nation. Systems of measurement, such as economic growth and technological advancement, while important, should not be considered more important than measurements reflective of societal well-being, ethical governance, and communal harmony. A truly successful nation is not just one that is powerful or wealthy but one that fosters compassion, justice, and a shared commitment to the greater good. If we Americans, the engine that runs our democracy, commit to ethical renewal, we can create a society where justice, integrity, and unity prevail.

In considering the insights of Jean Bethke Elshtain and Nancy J. Hirschmann, it is important to recognize that the tension between personal freedom and collective responsibility is not just relegated to an academic debate. The tension is a foundational challenge for any society seeking moral and political integrity. Their work serves as a guidepost, urging us to acknowledge that freedom, when disengaged from a sense of duty to others, risks becoming worthless and self-defeating.

This chapter has also examined how these thinkers compel us to restructure our understanding of autonomy, not as a shield against obligation, but as a formation through which true agency is realized. If Americans are to navigate the complexities of modern governance, social justice, and moral responsibility, then we have an obligation to embrace a conception of freedom that is enriched by ethical engagement and communal accountability.

Our lesson to learn is clear: Americans face the challenge to resist the temptation to reduce freedom to mere individualism and, instead, cultivate a vision of liberty that honors both personal agency and the moral imperatives that connect us together as one body. Only by doing so can we forge an American way of life that is both just and sustainable, a society in which freedom is not simply a right but a shared and upheld principle.

Epilogue

NO MORE DISGUISES

This closing echoes the Prologue: Selling an image to attain power, authority, and prominence has long been a tradition tied to achieving credibility, relevance, and value. But performance must end if our society is to liberate itself from the patterns that have led to the moral breakdown of our predecessors. No more masks. No more polished disingenuousness. The time has arrived for us to show up whole, even if that means showing up imperfect. It is important to remember that the character trait *accountability* is the confession of imperfection.

Our relationships, and certainly our society, cannot prosper or sustain themselves through means that portray a carefully staged existence. For lasting and meaningful longevity, our nation is in need of real people, living with real purpose. Our society requires men and women who see no need to live their lives behind illusions, who have no further desire to pretend, posture, or perform. When we honestly examine our interactions with one another, we are drowning in fabricated images, and yet we remain thirsty and starving for authenticity.

The challenge to morally elevate our nation, its communities, or even our family structures is impossible if we remain hidden behind delicately constructed roles. The truth is, we are not here to impress one another. But we are here to influence one another in an exemplary manner, to personify substantive character. And that begins when an individual can step fully into the best version of who they inherently are—a person of integrity, wisdom, love, and the capacity to lead and shape.

The central message of this book has consistently been this: to help an individual recognize, develop, and practice the best qualities they inherently possess. That truth, for each and every one of us, is not something to invent. It is something we are called to reveal. And when society encourages that process, we all benefit from this collective effort.

That is the art of unification. It begins within, but it does not end there. It calls us to look beyond ourselves, to stand uncovered not just for personal healing, but for the healing of our nation. Because once that truth is personally discovered, performance becomes pointless. What remains is real presence. And in that presence, we rediscover each other. We reconnect. We unify. It is time to live. And it is time to live *together*, unmasked, unshaken, and undivided.

Lorenzo D. Leonard

ABOUT THE AUTHOR

Lorenzo D. Leonard is a writer and thought leader who is committed to resolving societal problems by addressing the root cause of the social symptoms of injustice, oppression, gender inequality, racism, classism, and ageism through his work.

The deep insights and challenging rhetoric in *The Art of Unification* seek to awaken the reader to the systemic issues plaguing our nation while fostering deeper understanding, honest reflection, and a willingness to initiate meaningful and lasting change.

His previous works include *The True Holy War* (2009), *Empires vs. Coalitions* (2013), *At First Glance* (2021), *Rules of Engagement* (2021), *To the Issue of Credibility, Relevance, and Value: Educate to Character* (2022), and *Trust the Confession* (2023).

You can learn more about his work at www.pugetsoundbooks.com.

www.ingramcontent.com/pod-product-compliance
Lightning Source LLC
Chambersburg PA
CBHW070111030426
42335CB00016B/2112